Real World

Colouring Book

For Advanced Users & Adults

50 Images

**Created From Real Life Photos
For You To Colour As You Please.**

ISBN 978-0-359-93605-2

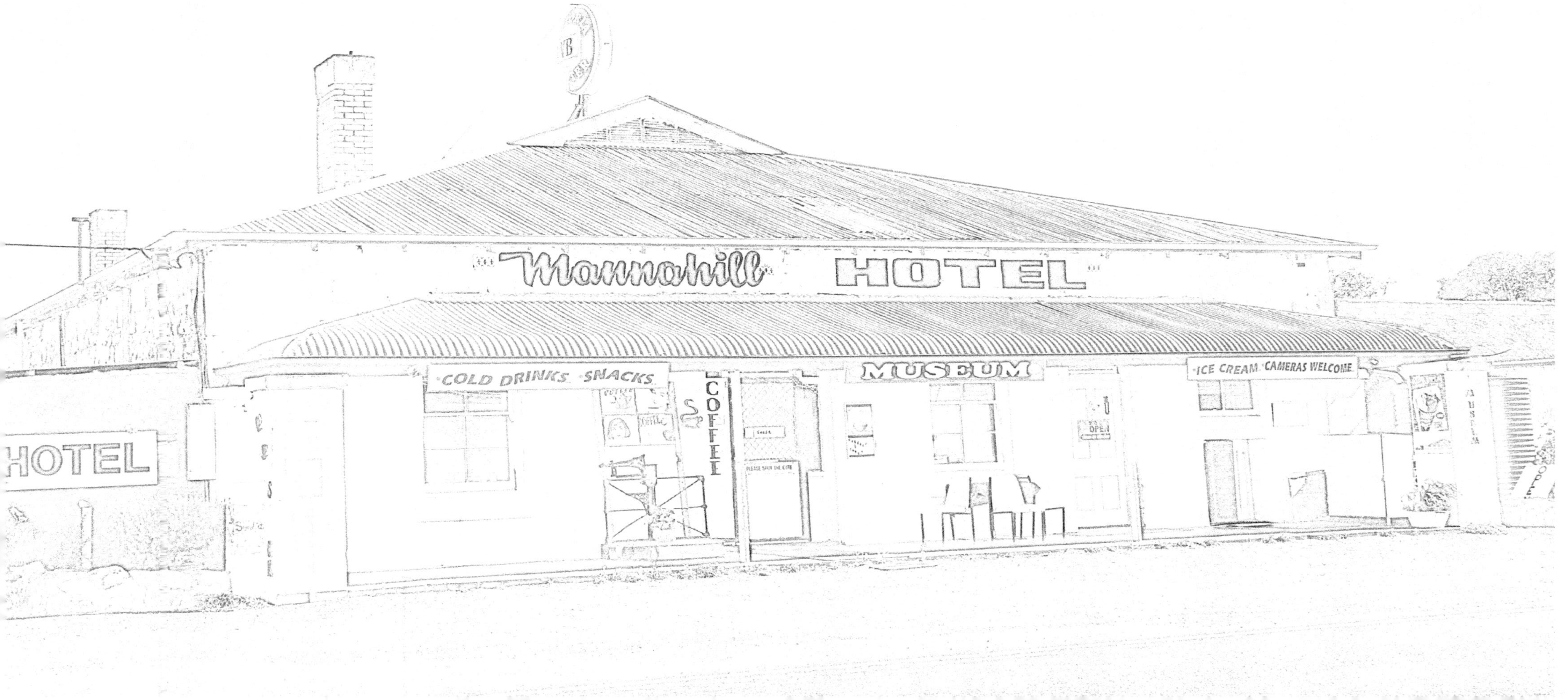
Mannahill HOTEL
COLD DRINKS SNACKS
COFFEE
MUSEUM
ICE CREAM CAMERAS WELCOME
OPEN
HOTEL

MANNAHILL

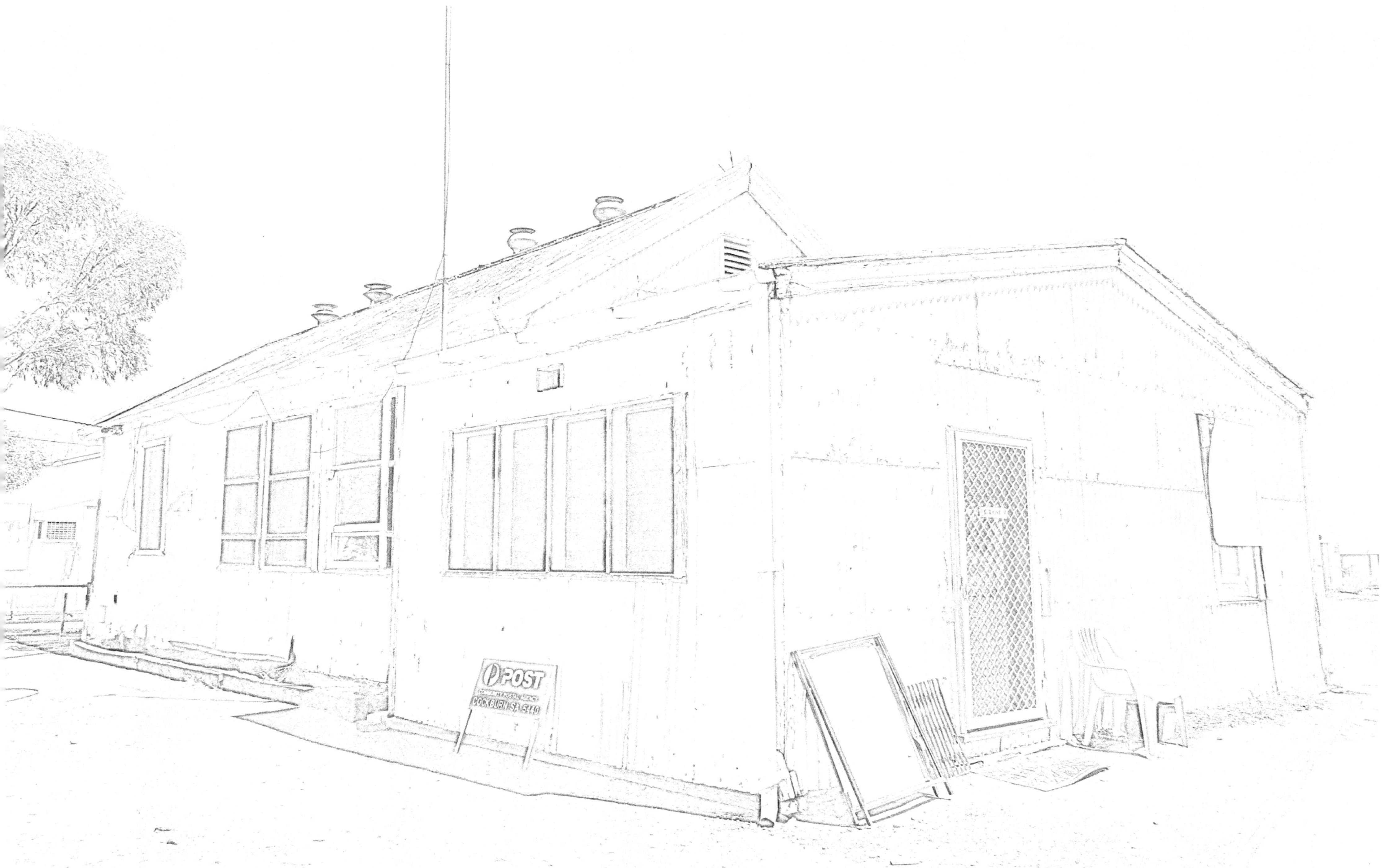
POST
COMMUNITY POSTAL AGENCY
COCKBURN SA 5440

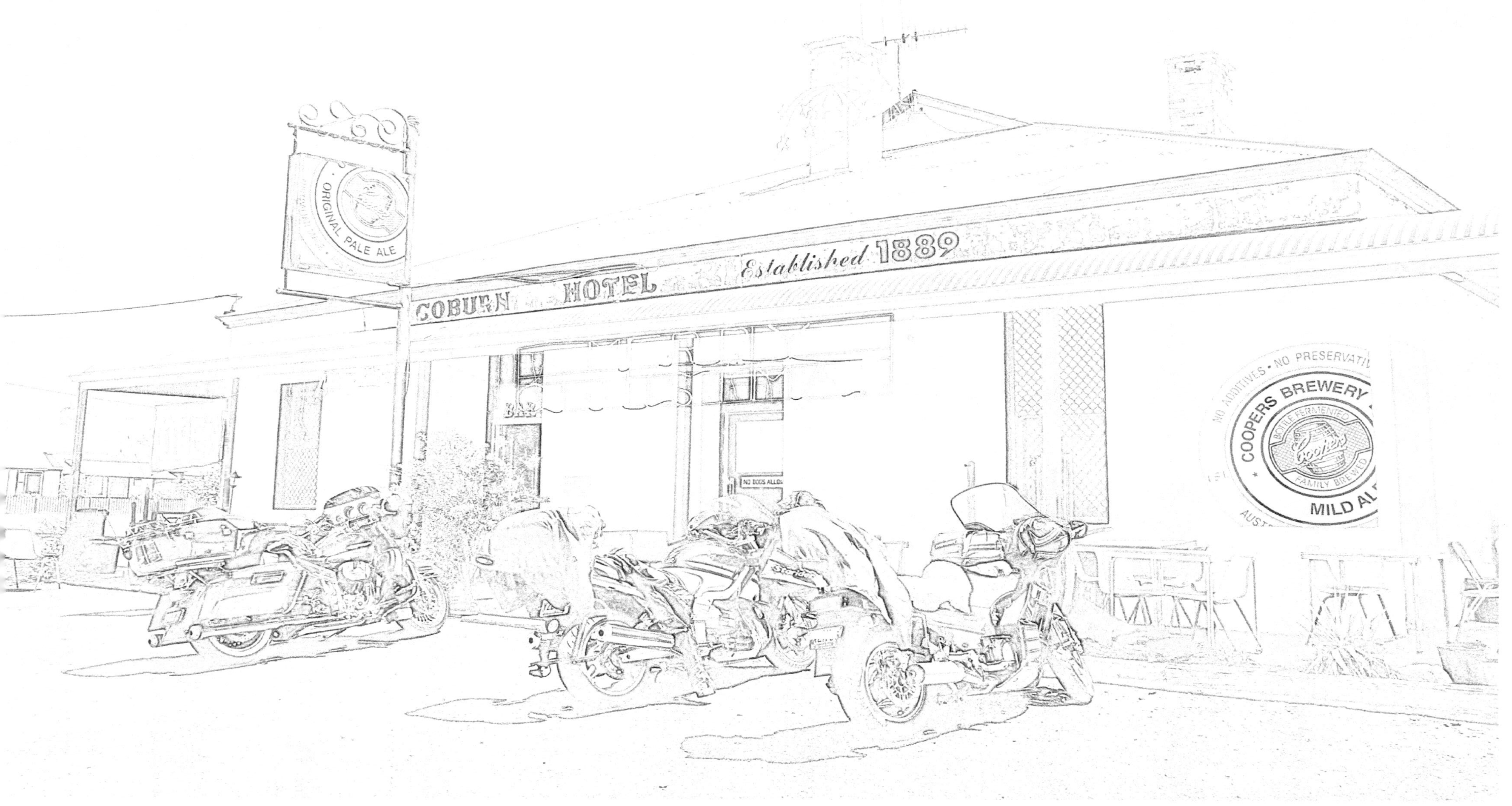
ORIGINAL PALE ALE
COBURN HOTEL
Established 1889
NO DOGS ALLOW
COOPERS BREWERY
NO ADDITIVES • NO PRESERVATIV
BOTTLE FERMENTED
FAMILY BREWED
MILD AL

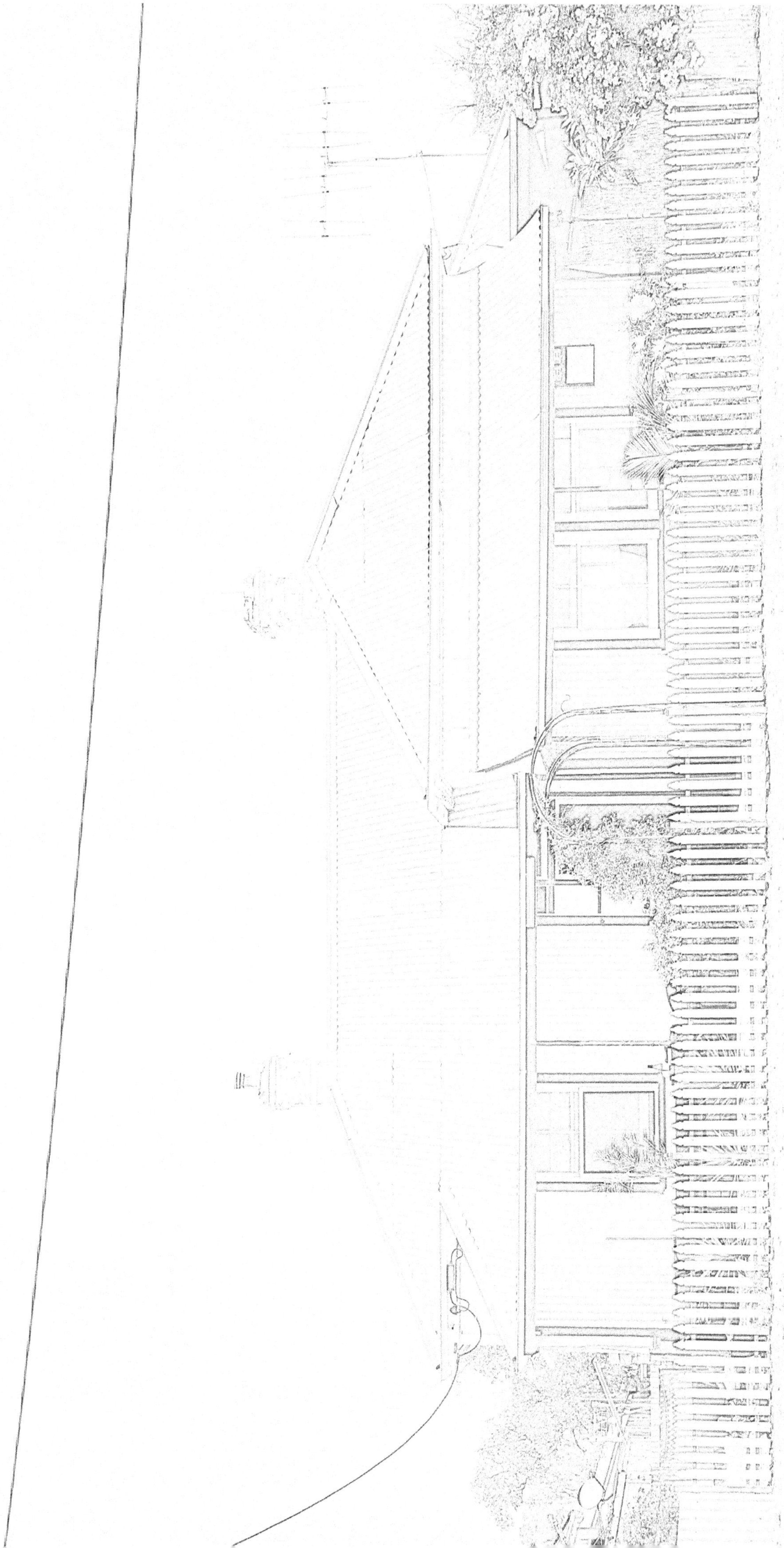

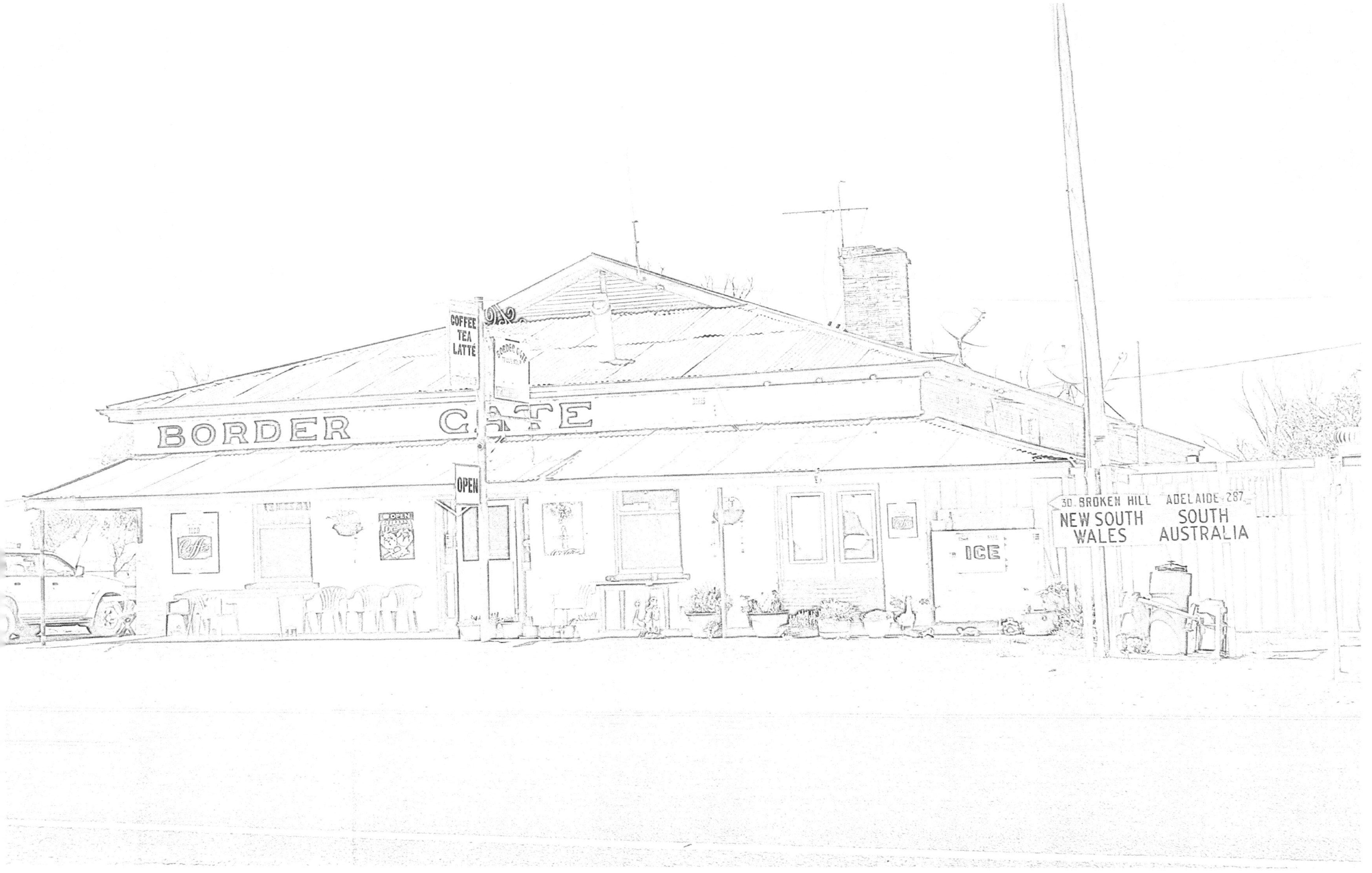
BORDER
COFFEE
TEA
LATTÉ
OPEN
ICE
30 BROKEN HILL
ADELAIDE 287
NEW SOUTH
WALES
SOUTH
AUSTRALIA

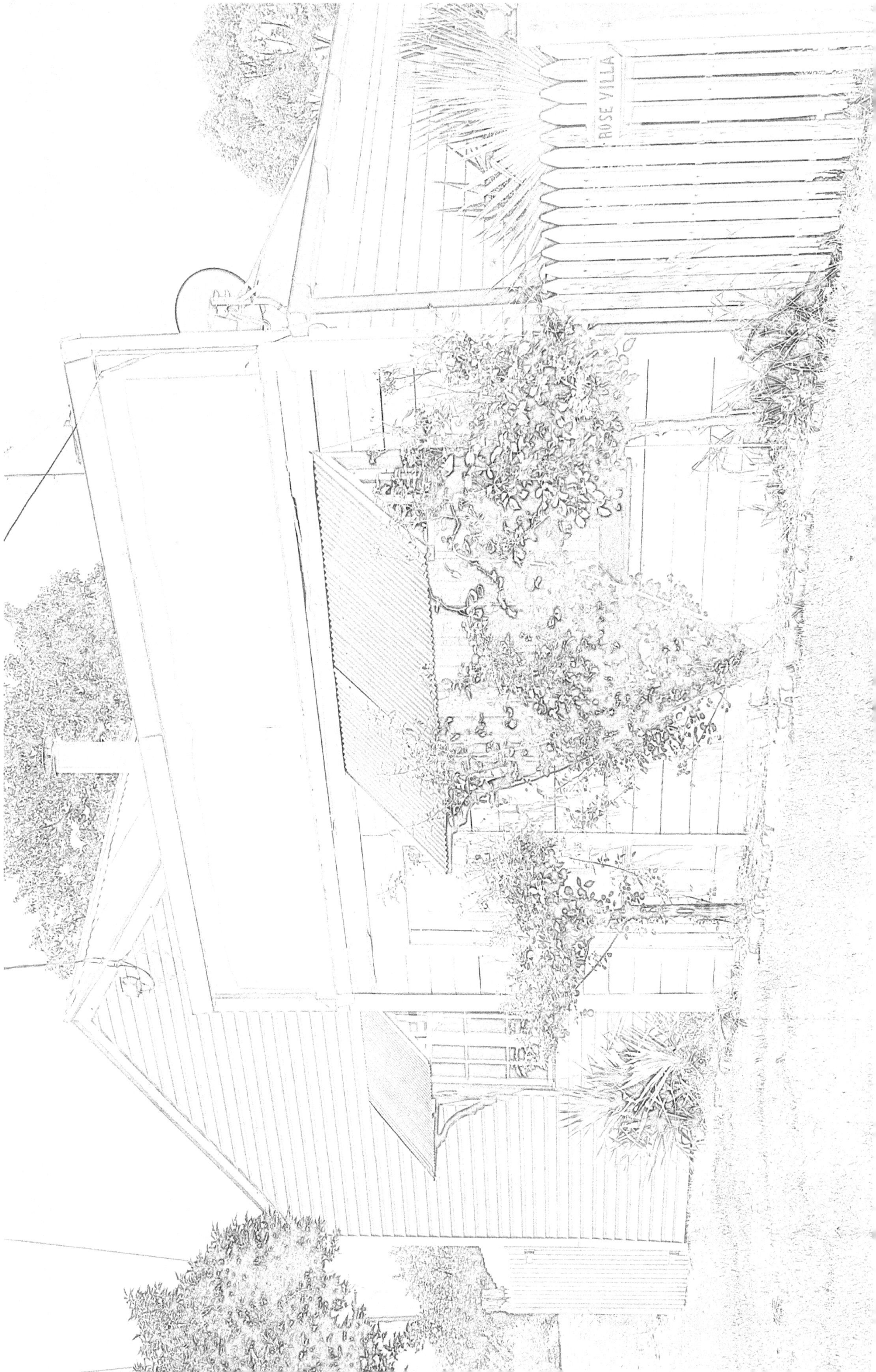
ROSE VILLA

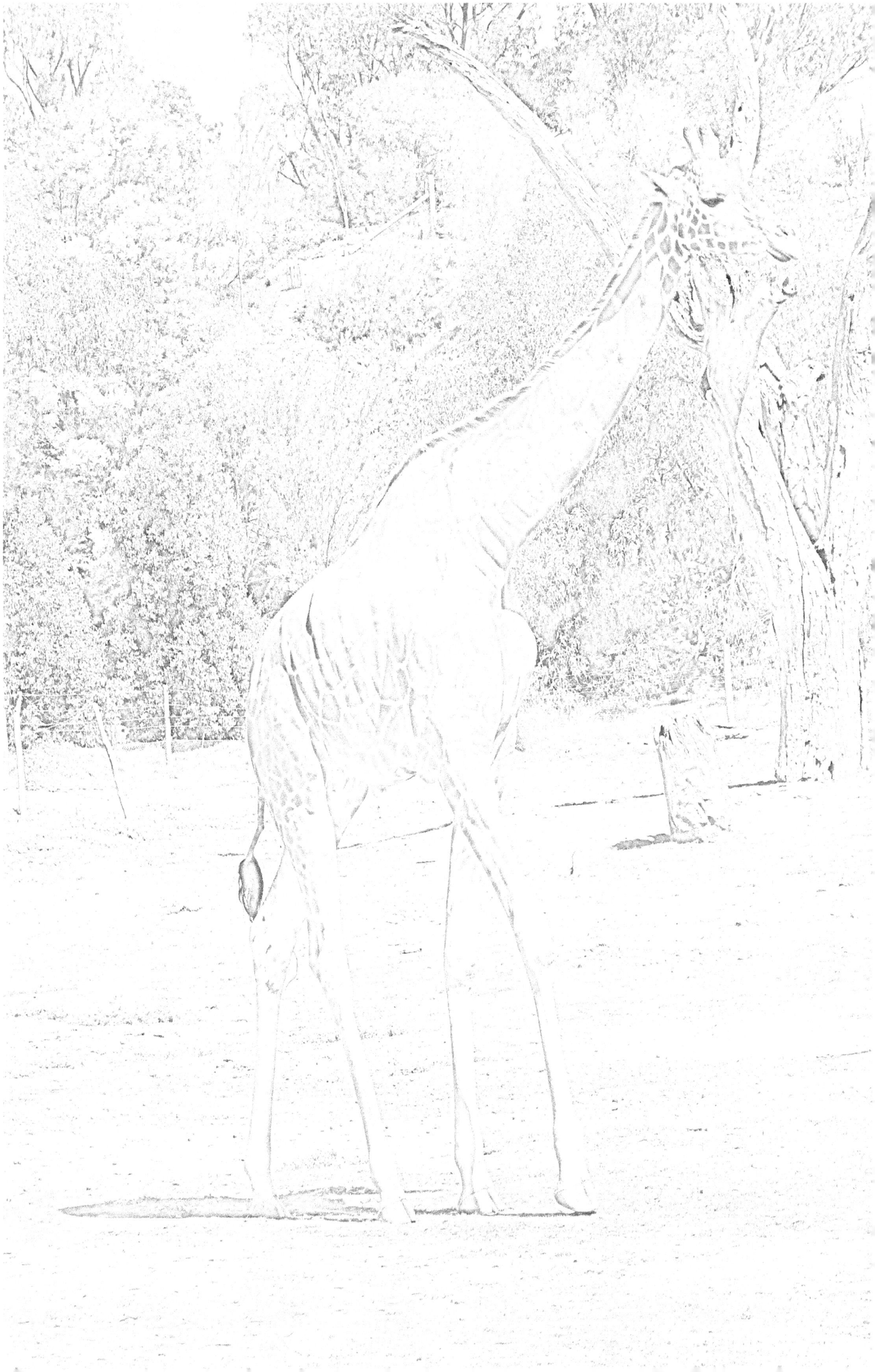

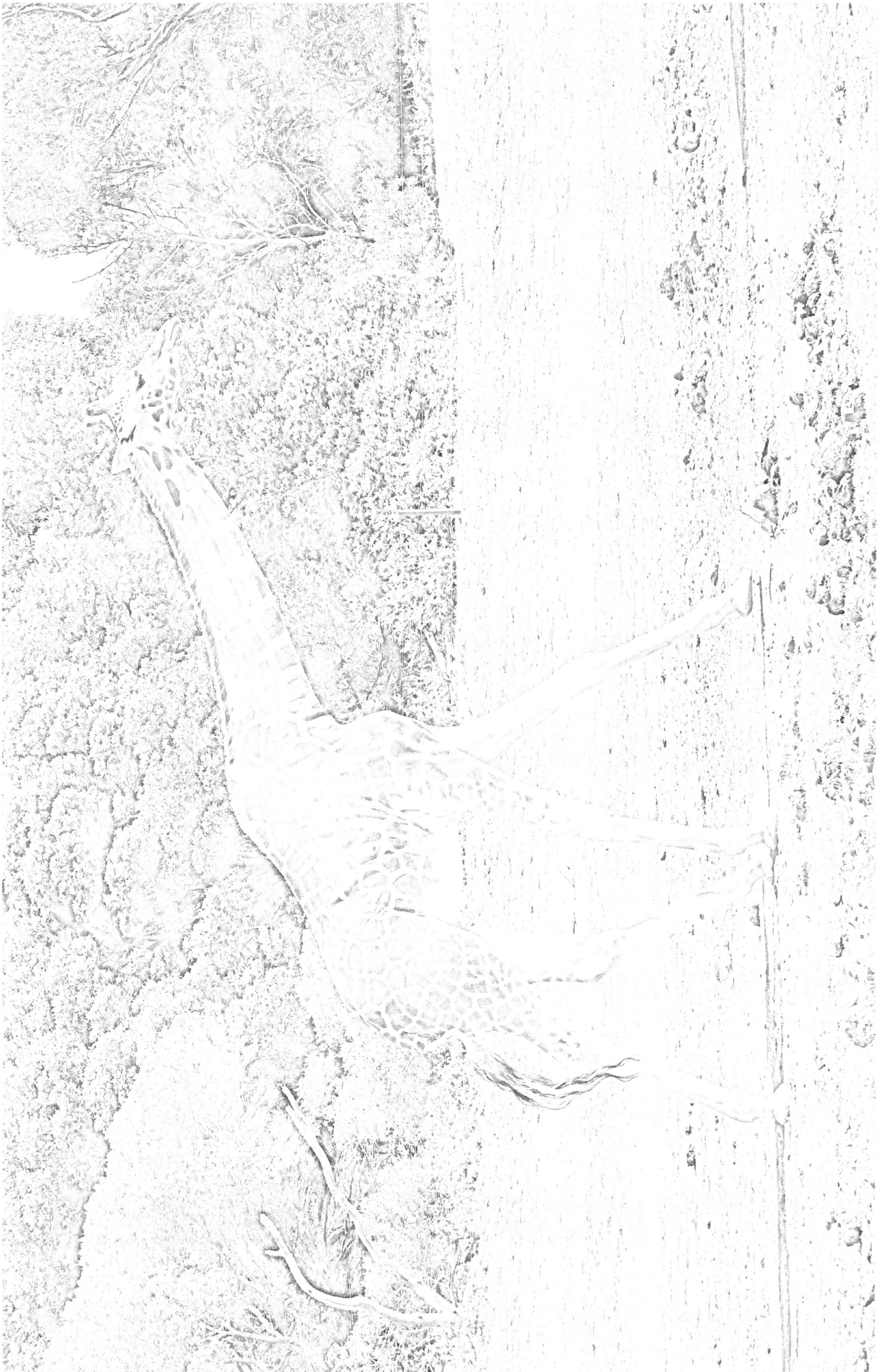

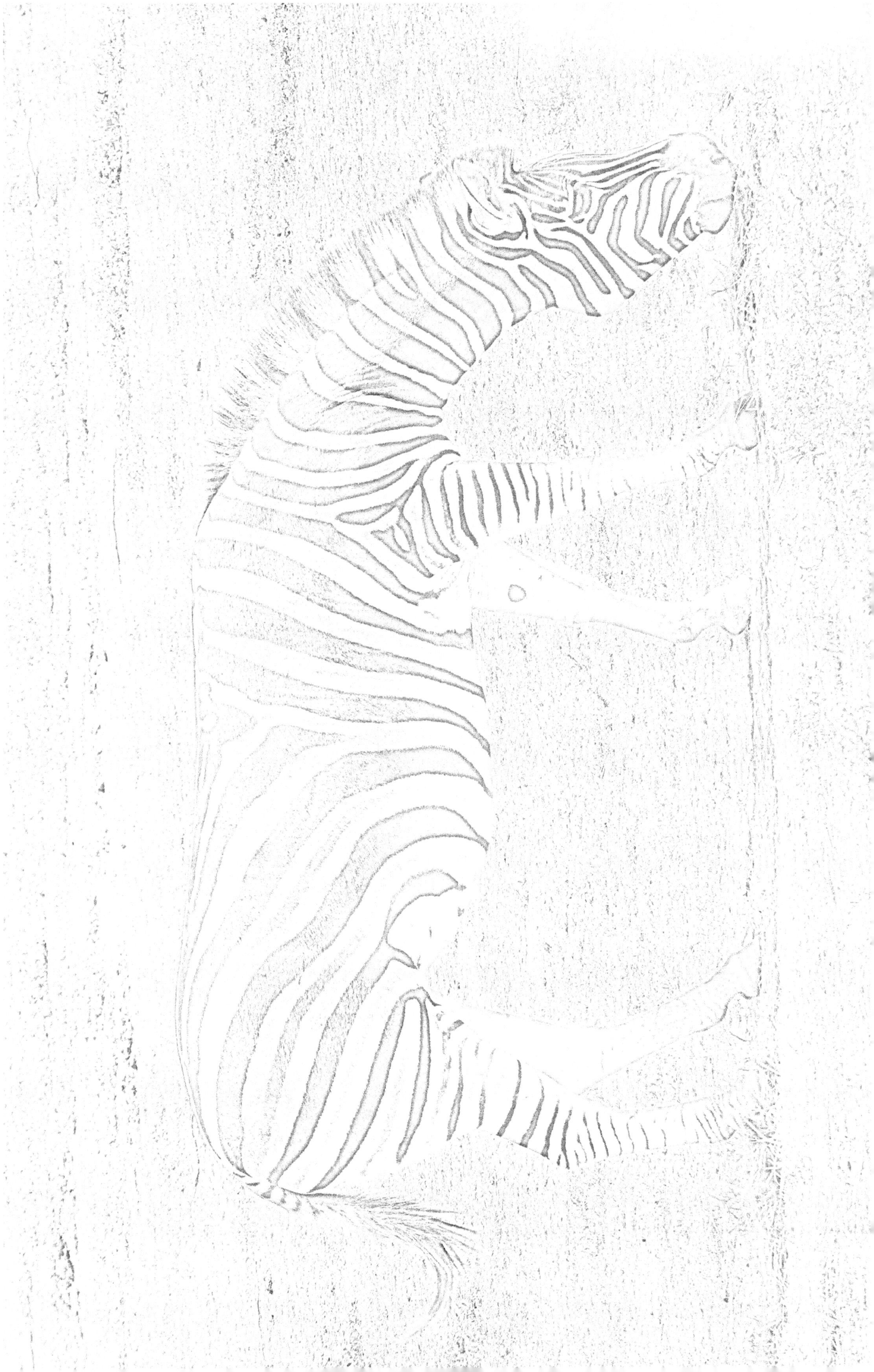

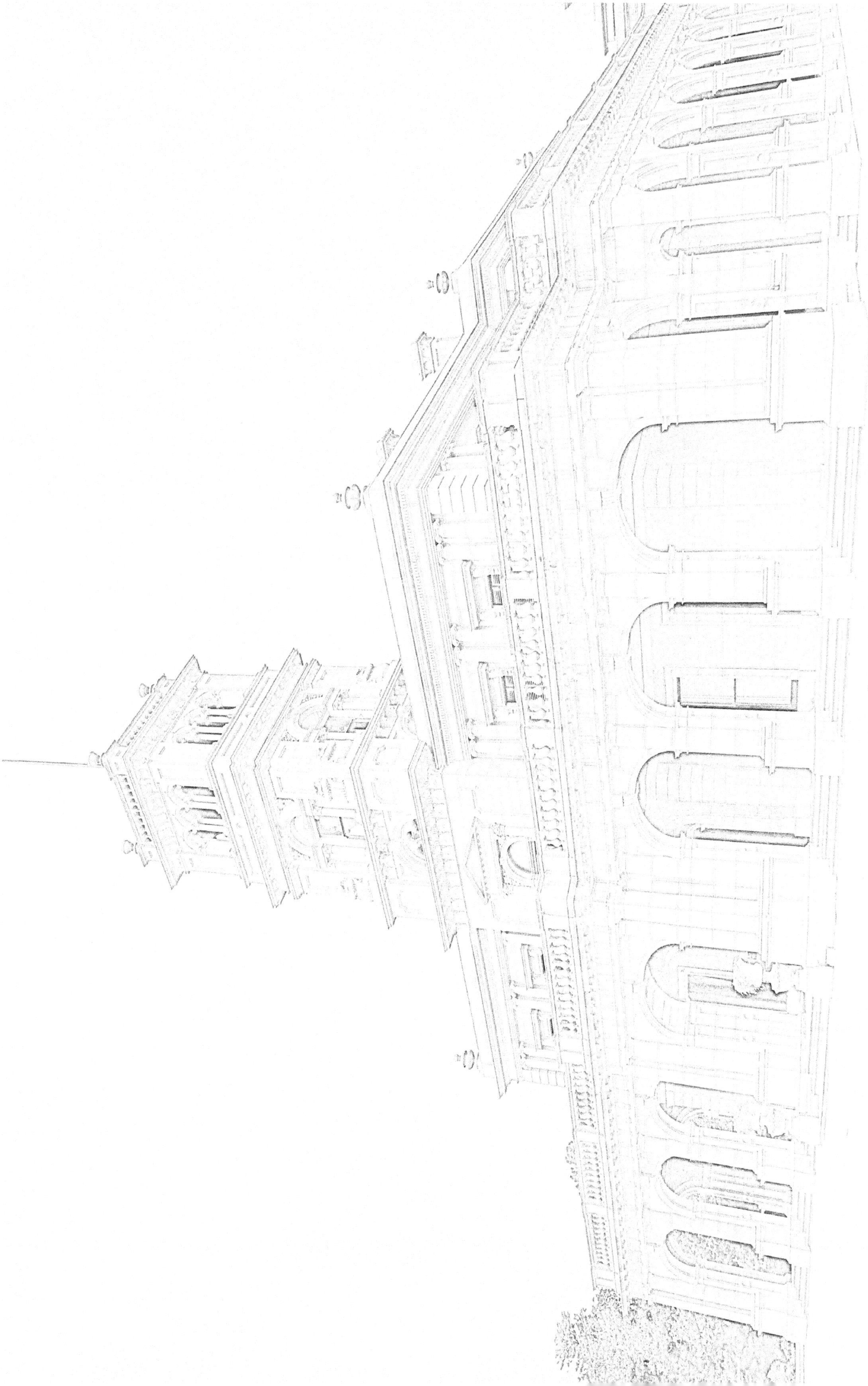

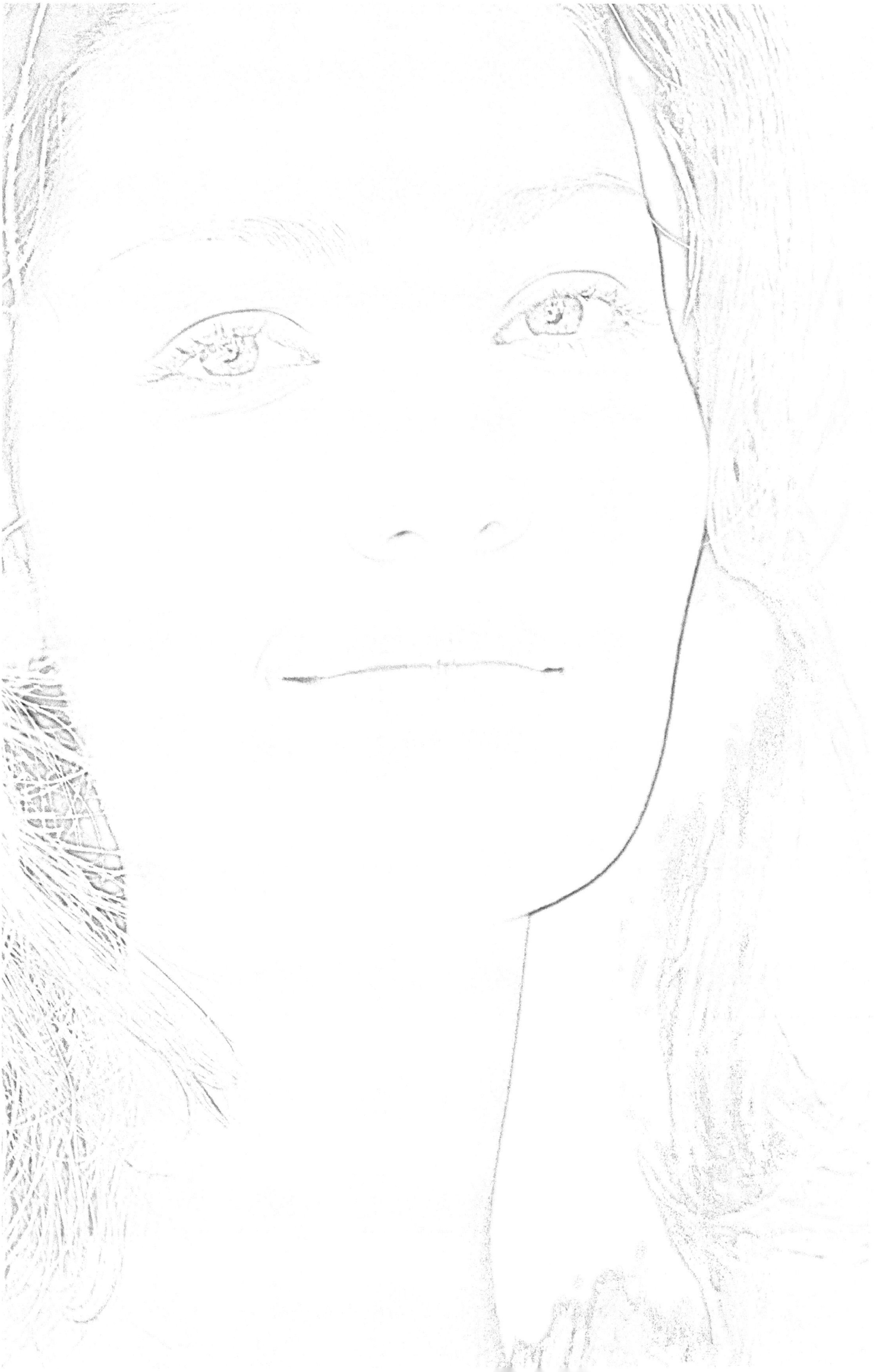

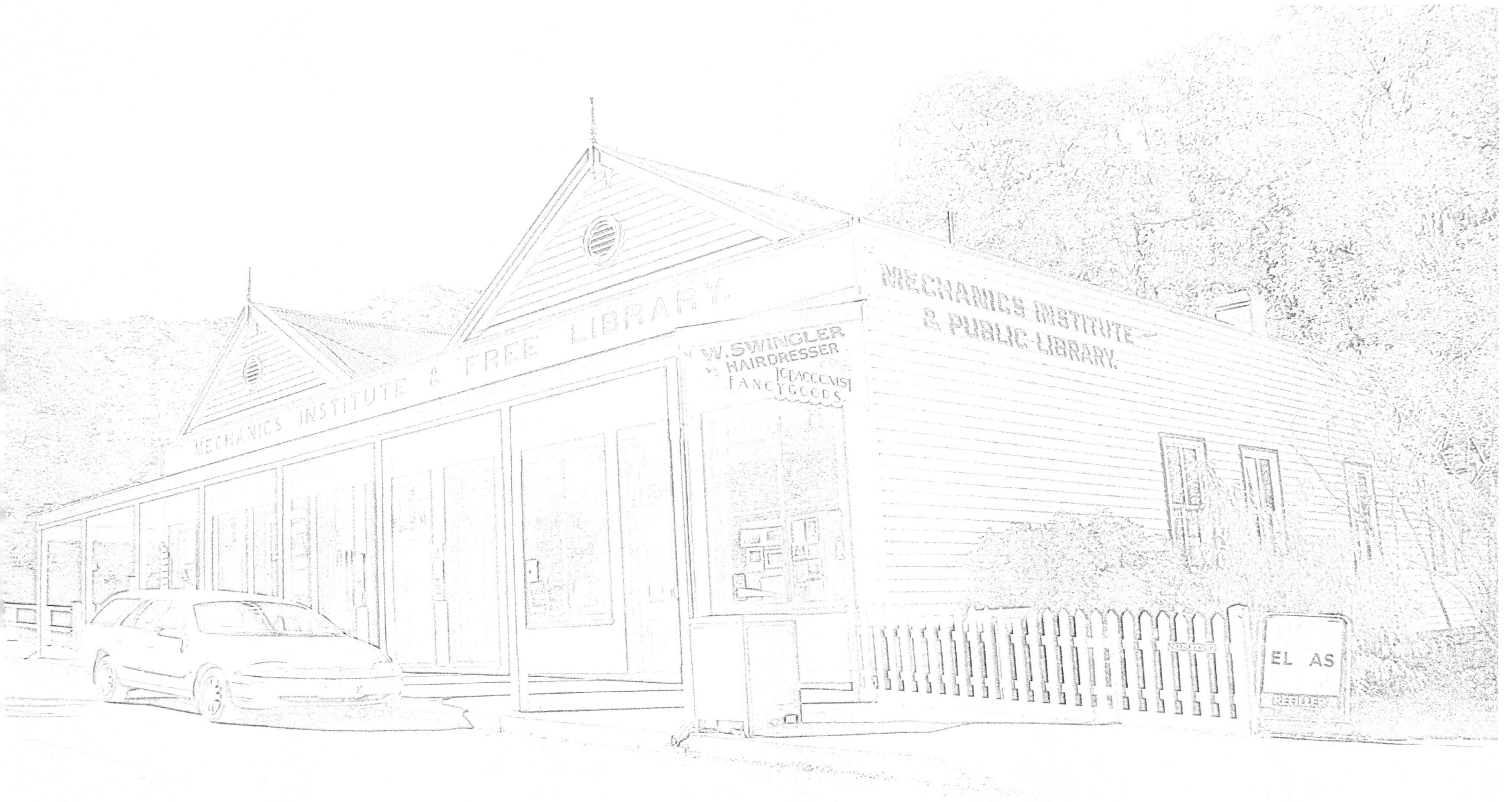
MECHANICS INSTITUTE & FREE LIBRARY.
W. SWINGLER
HAIRDRESSER
TOBACCONIST
FANCY GOODS.
MECHANICS INSTITUTE
& PUBLIC LIBRARY.
EL AS
REFILLER

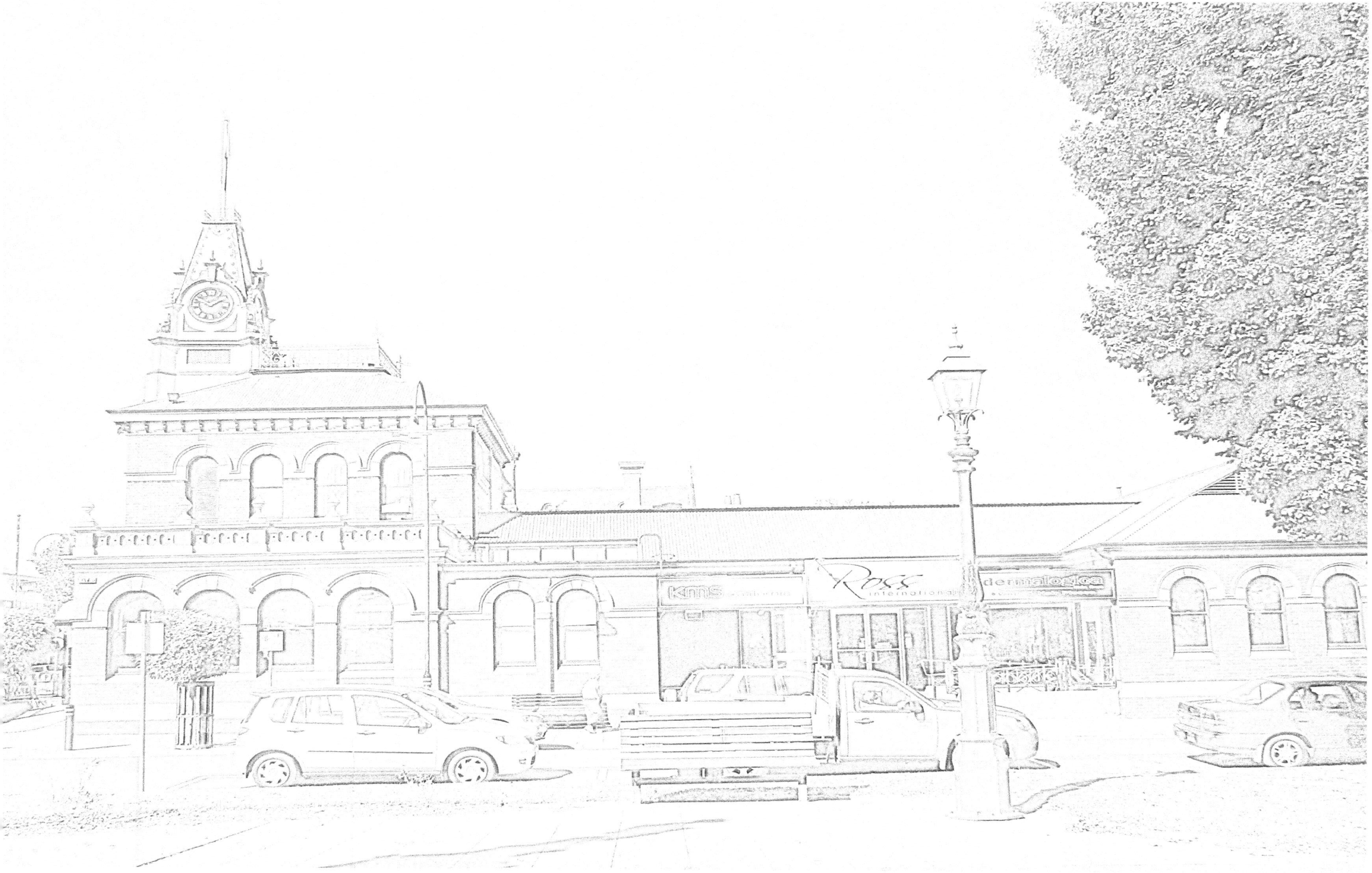
kms
Ross
international
dermalogica

TOWN HALL

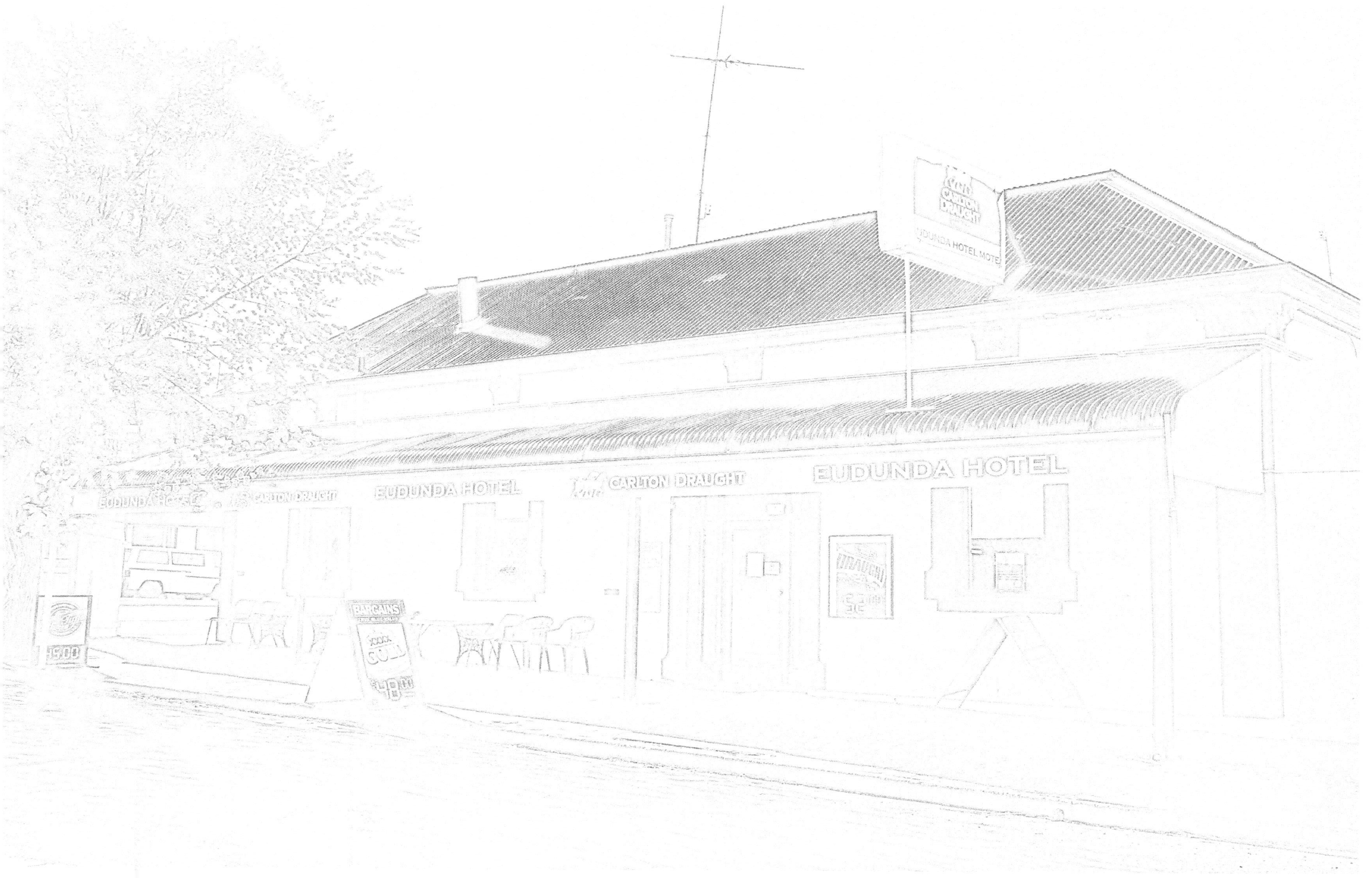
CARLTON DRAUGHT
EUDUNDA HOTEL MOTEL
EUDUNDA HOTEL
CARLTON DRAUGHT
EUDUNDA HOTEL
CARLTON DRAUGHT
EUDUNDA HOTEL
BARGAINS
XXXX GOLD

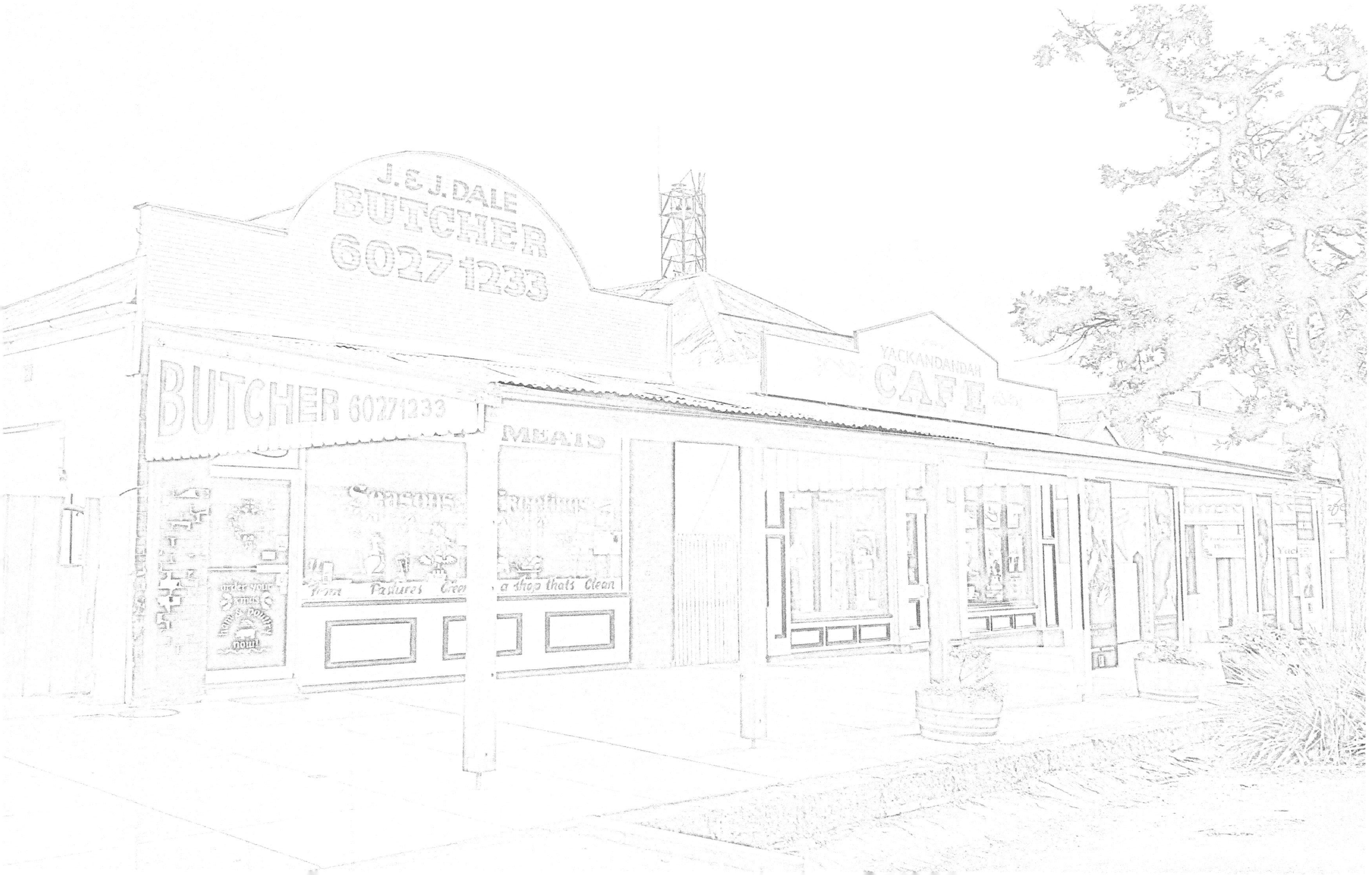
J. & J. DALE
BUTCHER
6027 1233
BUTCHER 60271233
MEATS
a shop thats Clean
YACKANDANDAH
CAFE

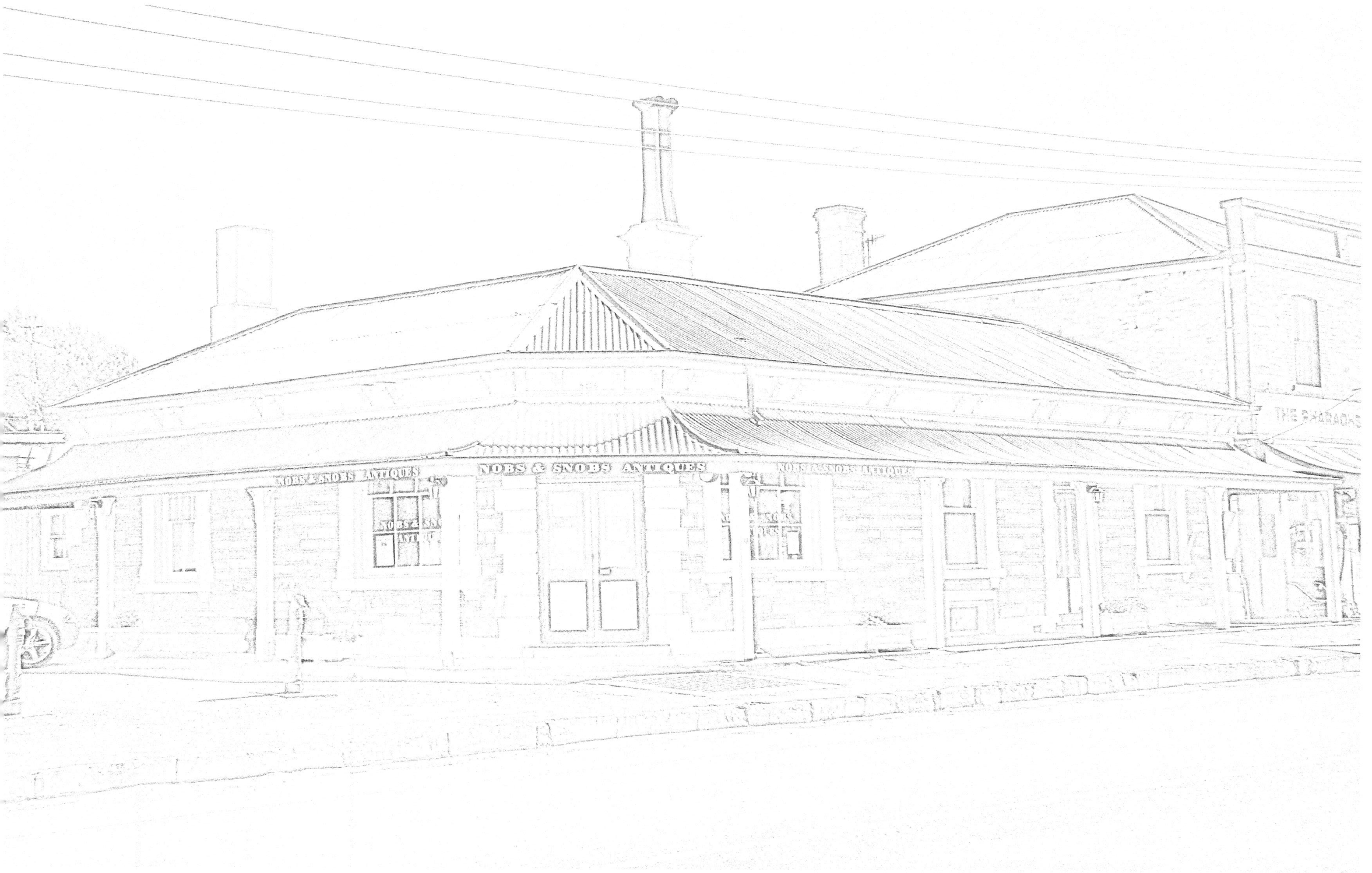
NOBS & SNOBS ANTIQUES
NOBS & SNOBS ANTIQUES
NOBS & SNOBS ANTIQUES

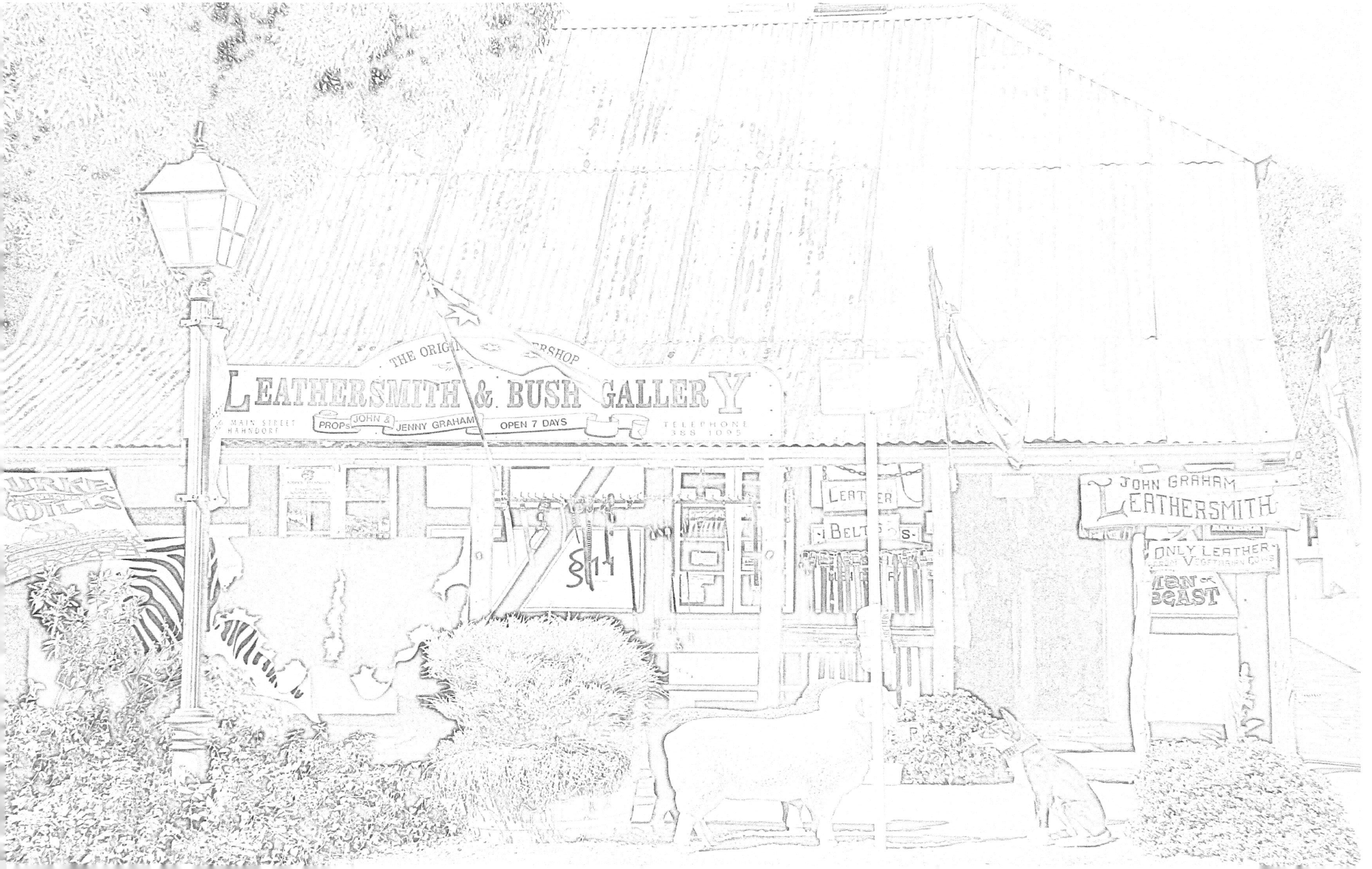
LEATHERSMITH & BUSH GALLERY
MAIN STREET HAHNDORF
PROPS JOHN & JENNY GRAHAM
OPEN 7 DAYS
TELEPHONE 388 1095
JOHN GRAHAM
LEATHERSMITH
ONLY LEATHER
MAN OR BEAST
LEATHER
BELTS

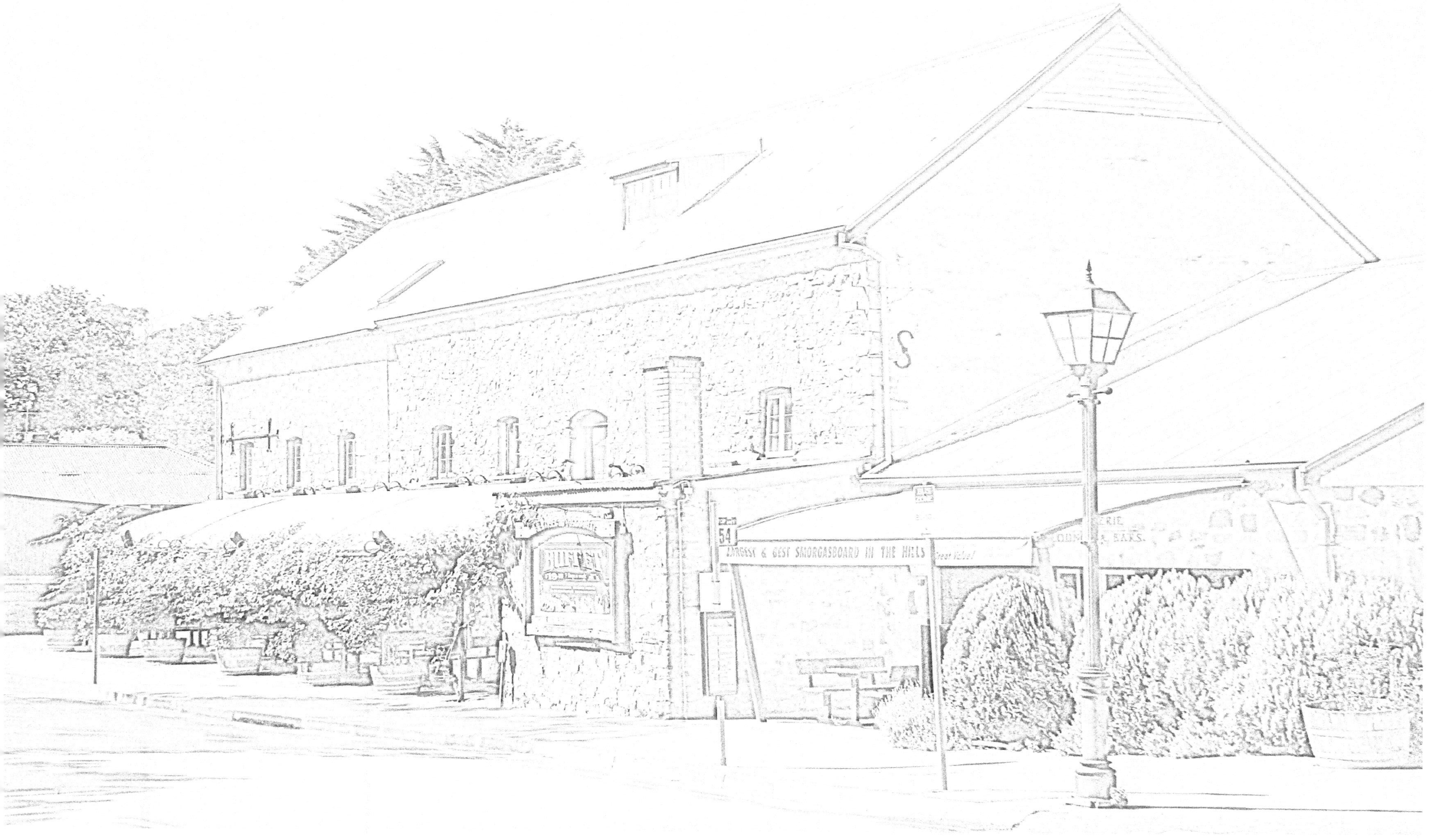
54
LARGEST & BEST SMORGASBOARD IN THE HILLS
Great Value!
BUFFET

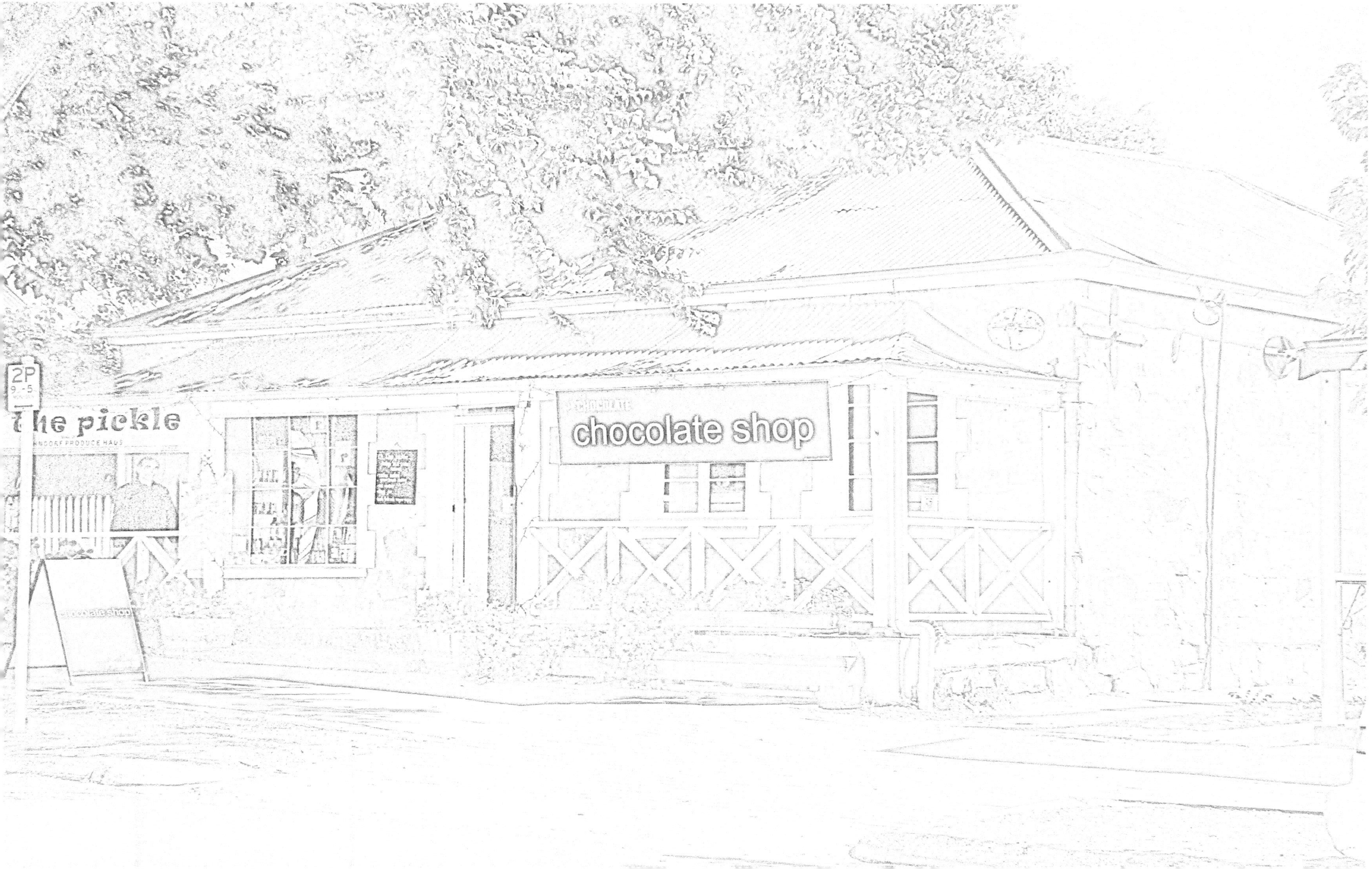
2P
the pickle
chocolate shop
chocolate shop

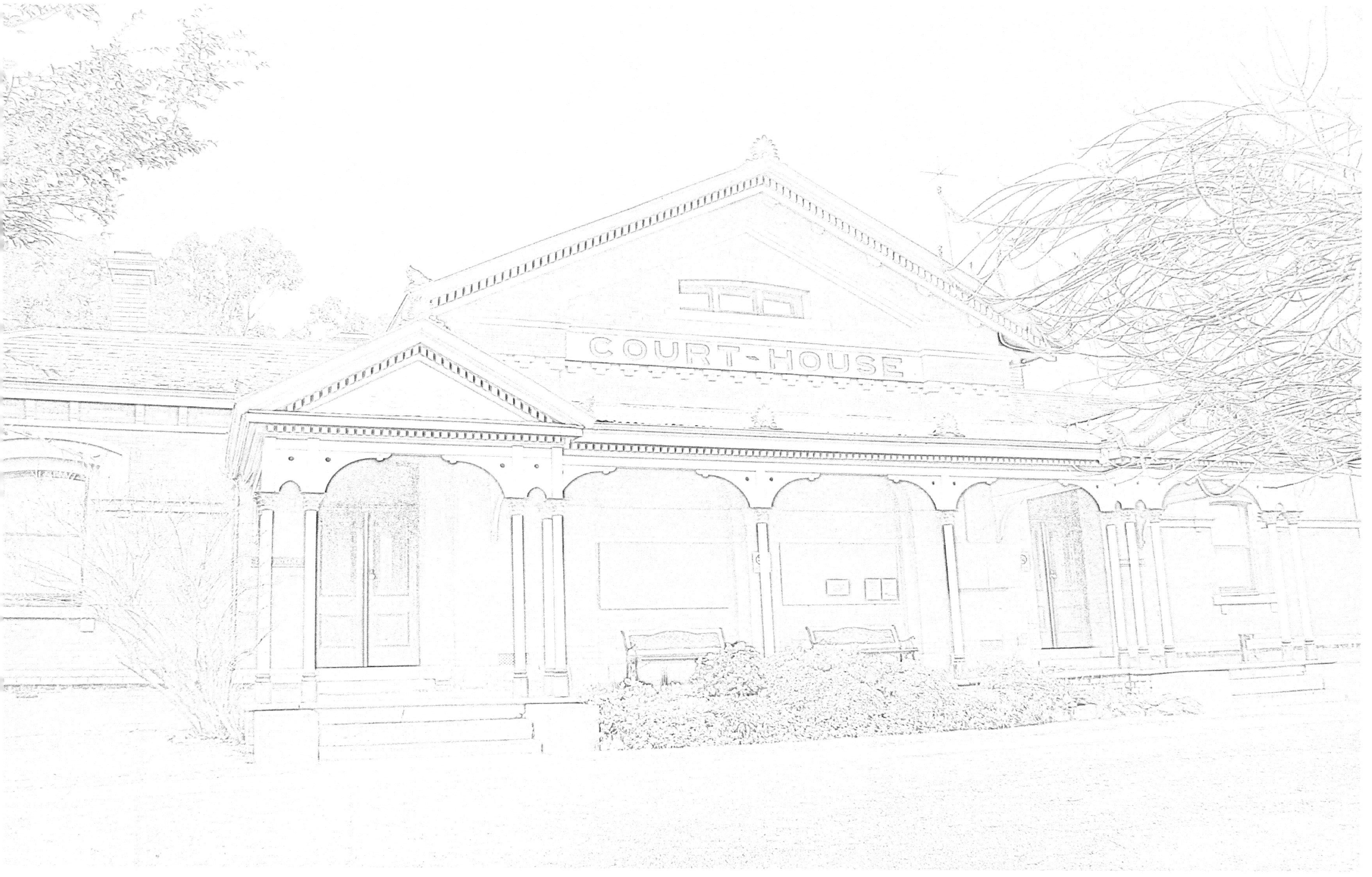
COURT-HOUSE

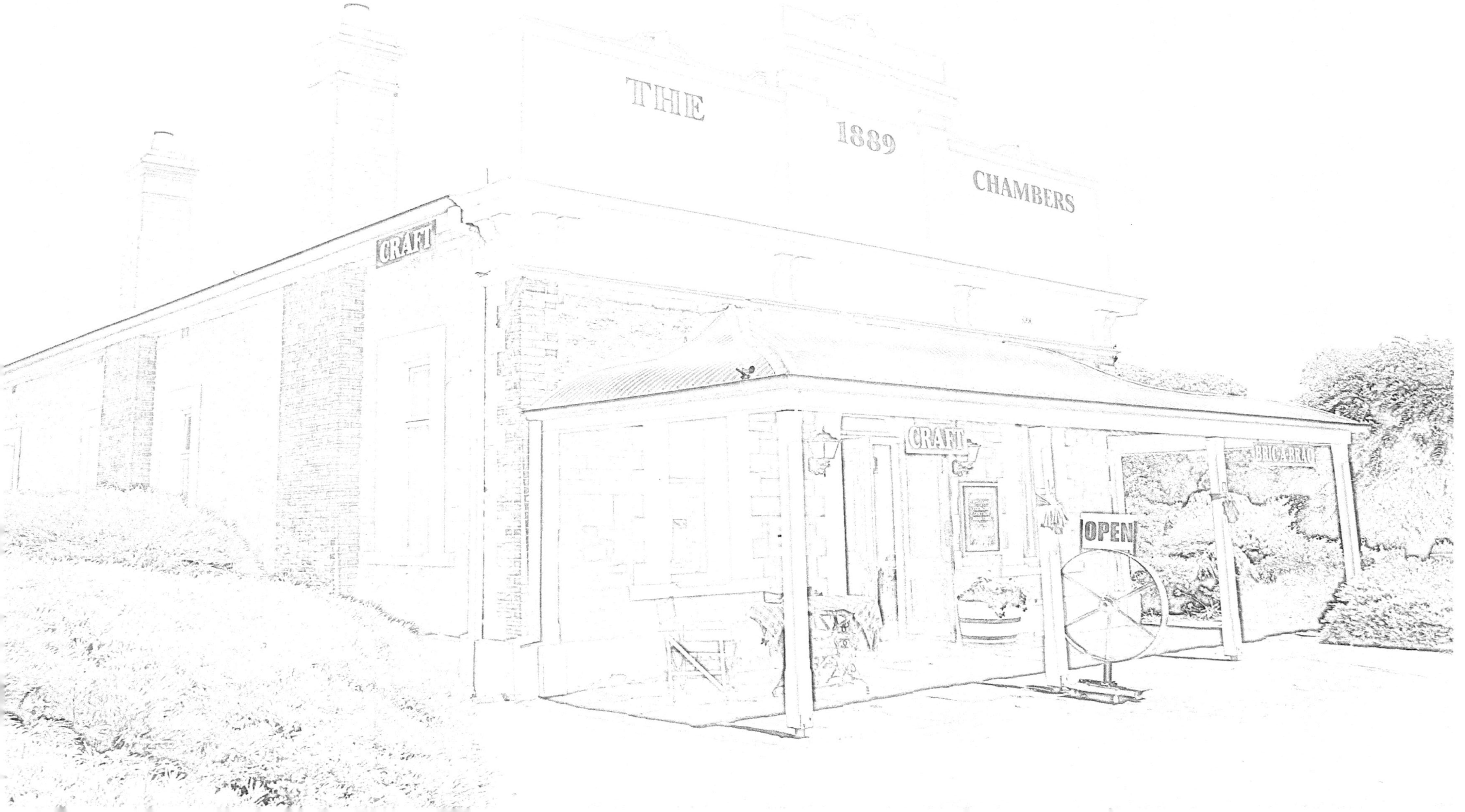
THE 1889 CHAMBERS
CRAFT
CRAFT
BRIC-A-BRAC
OPEN

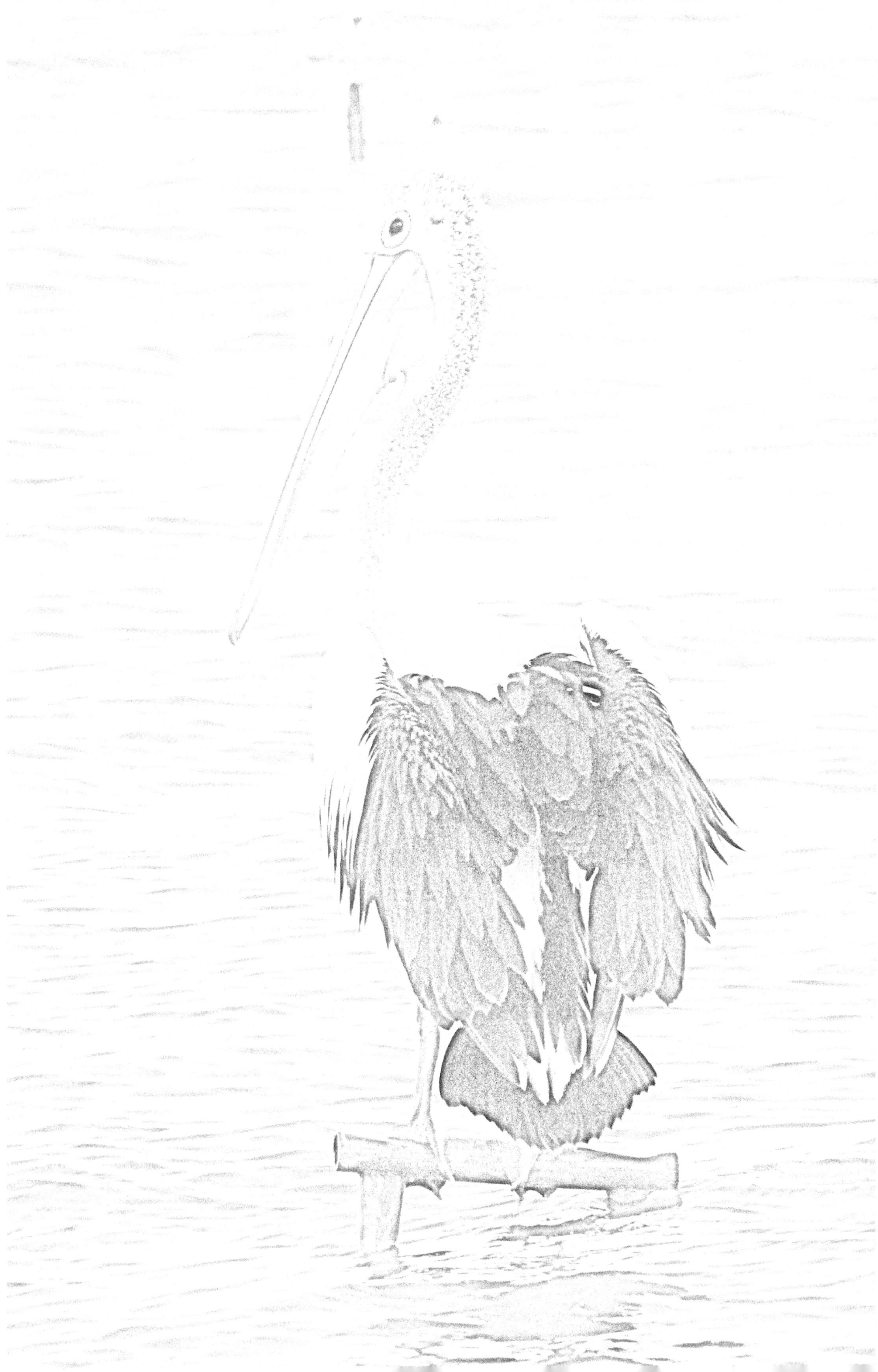

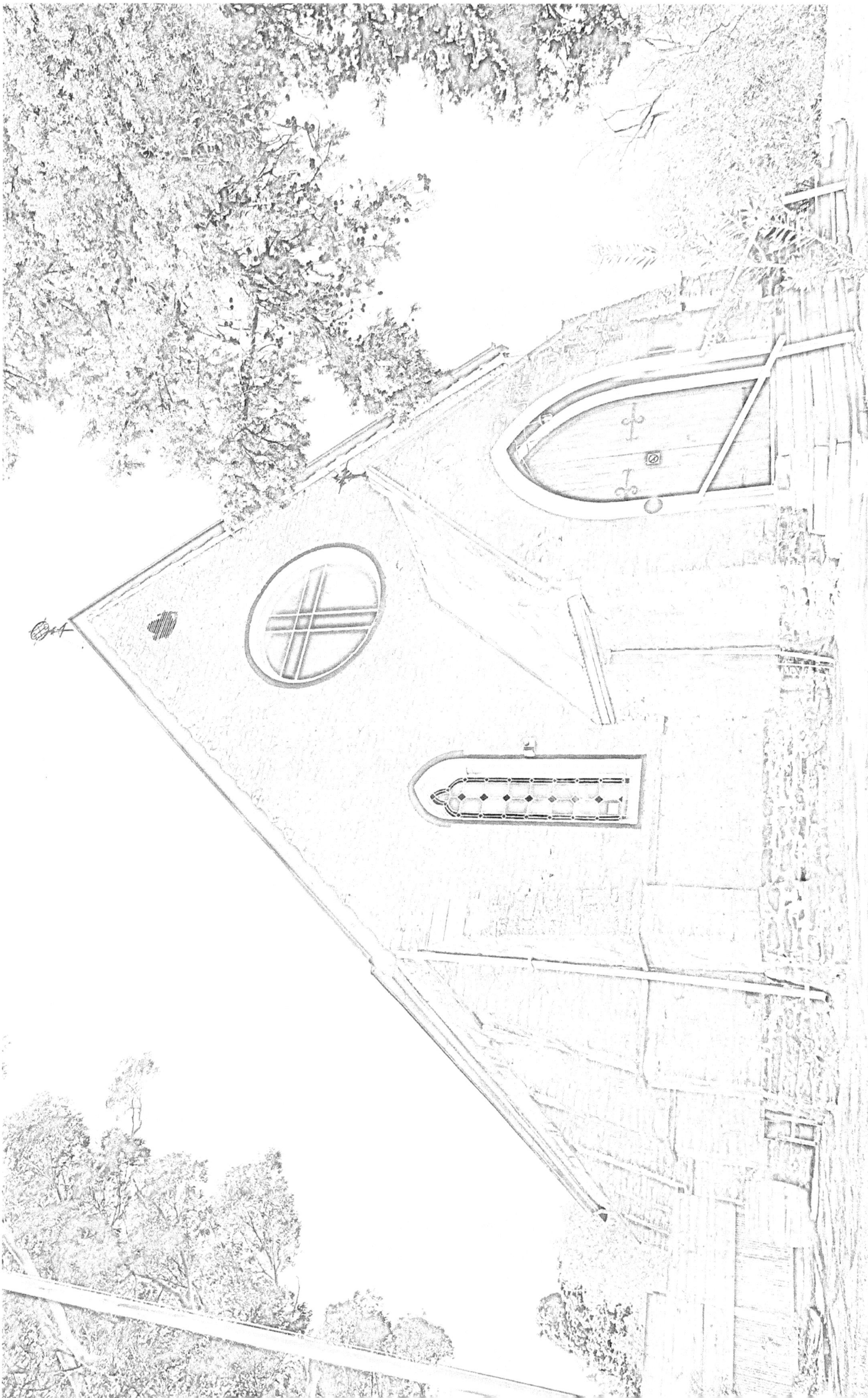

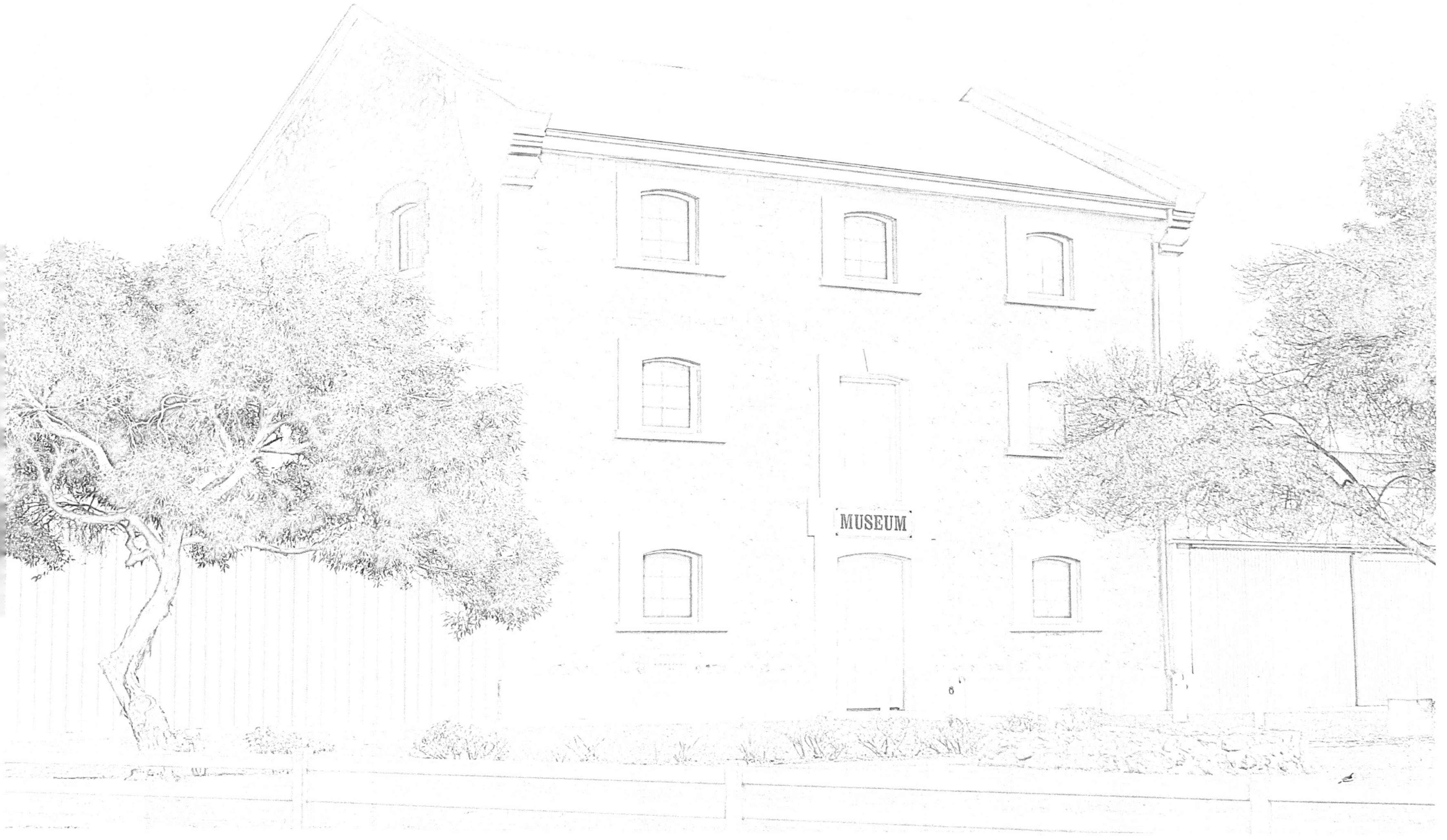
MUSEUM

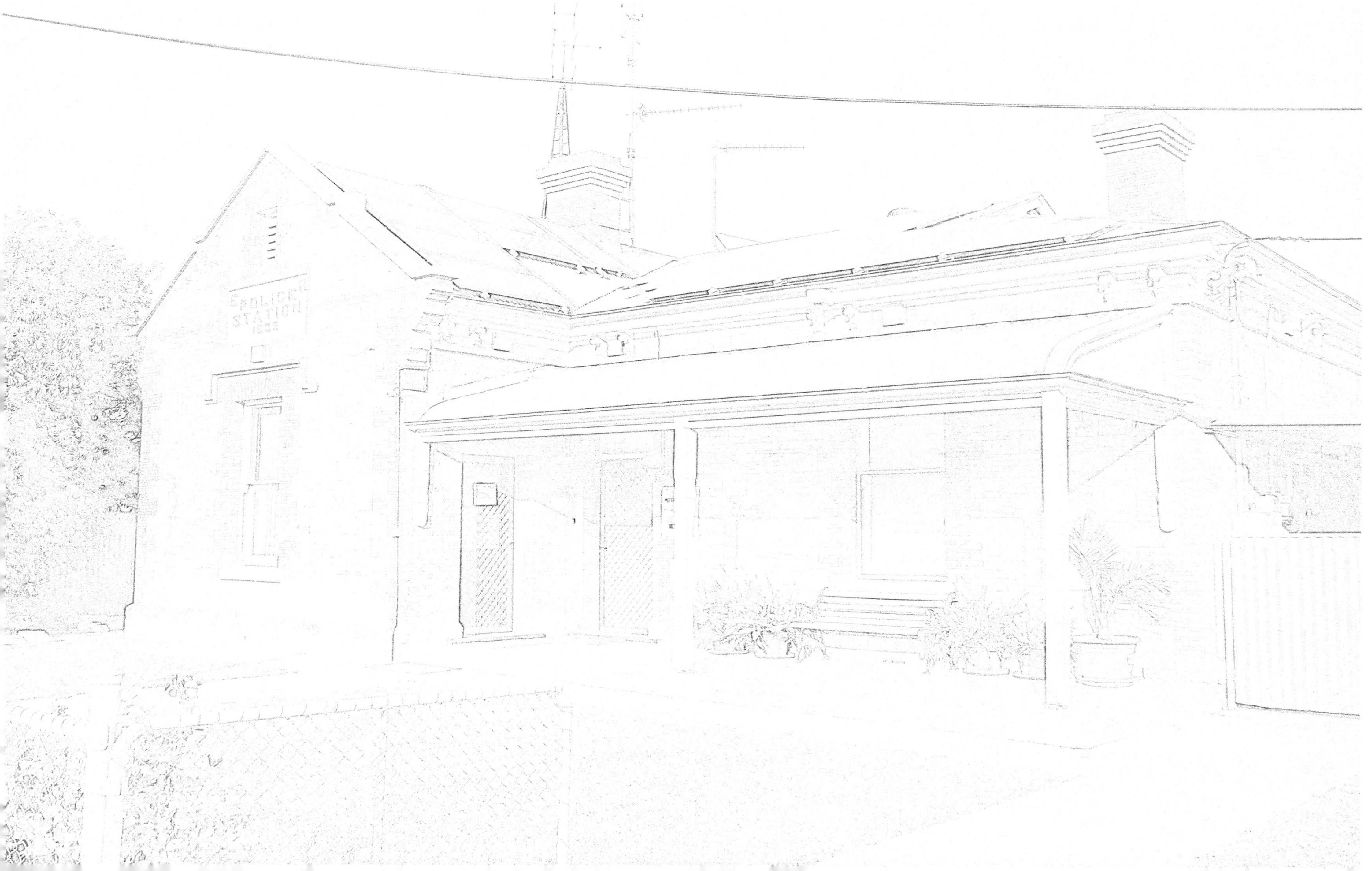
POLICE
STATION

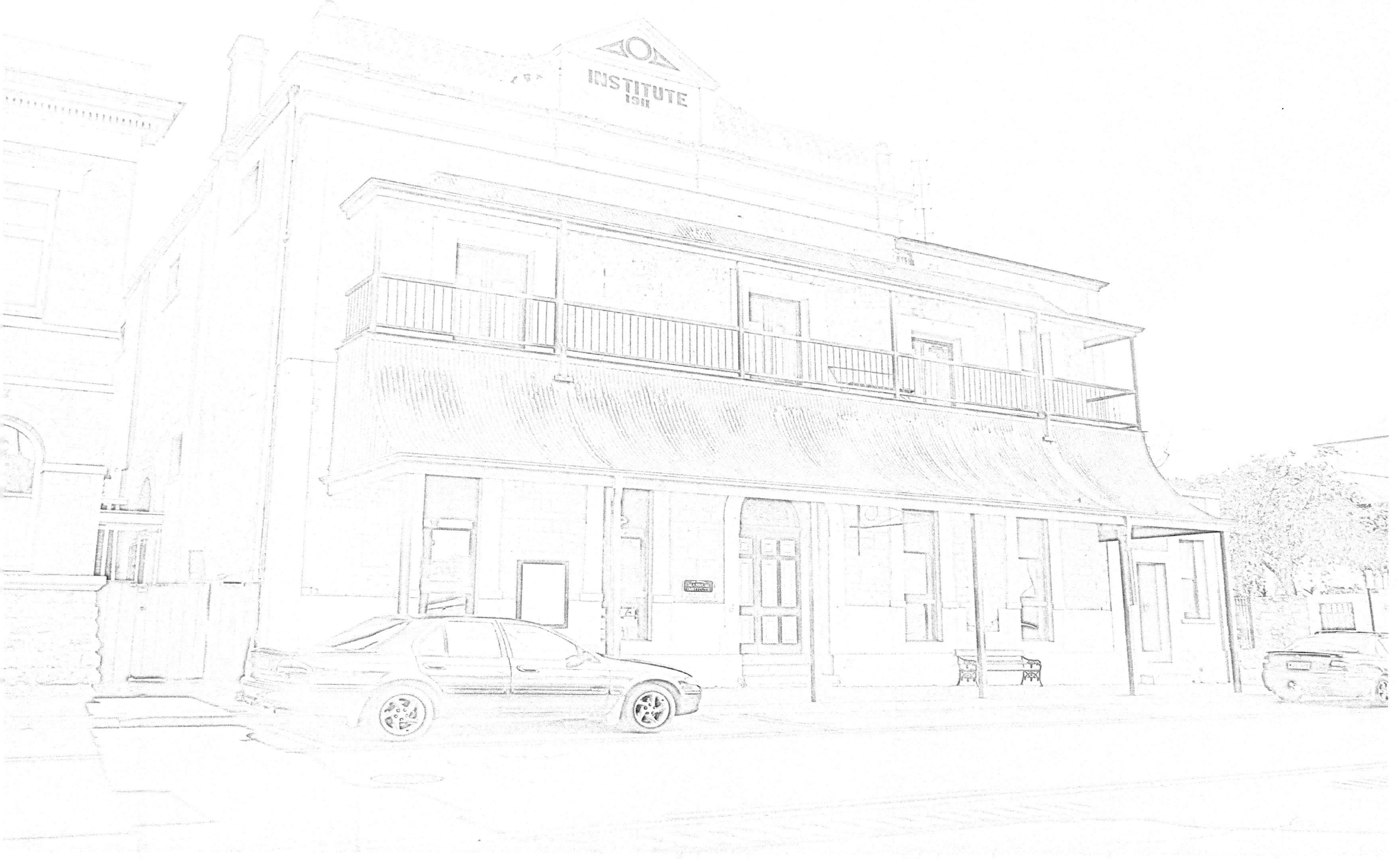
INSTITUTE
1911

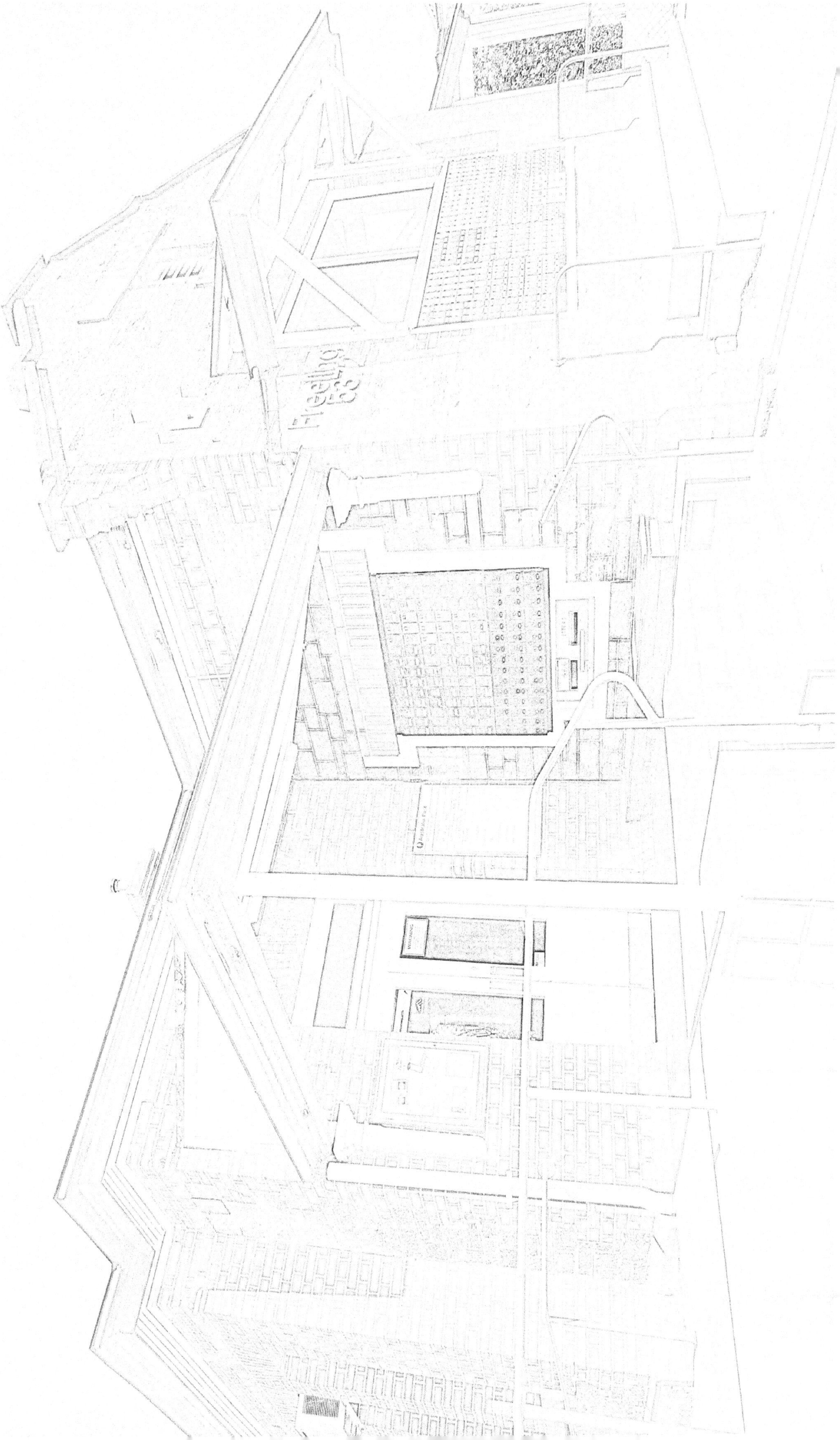

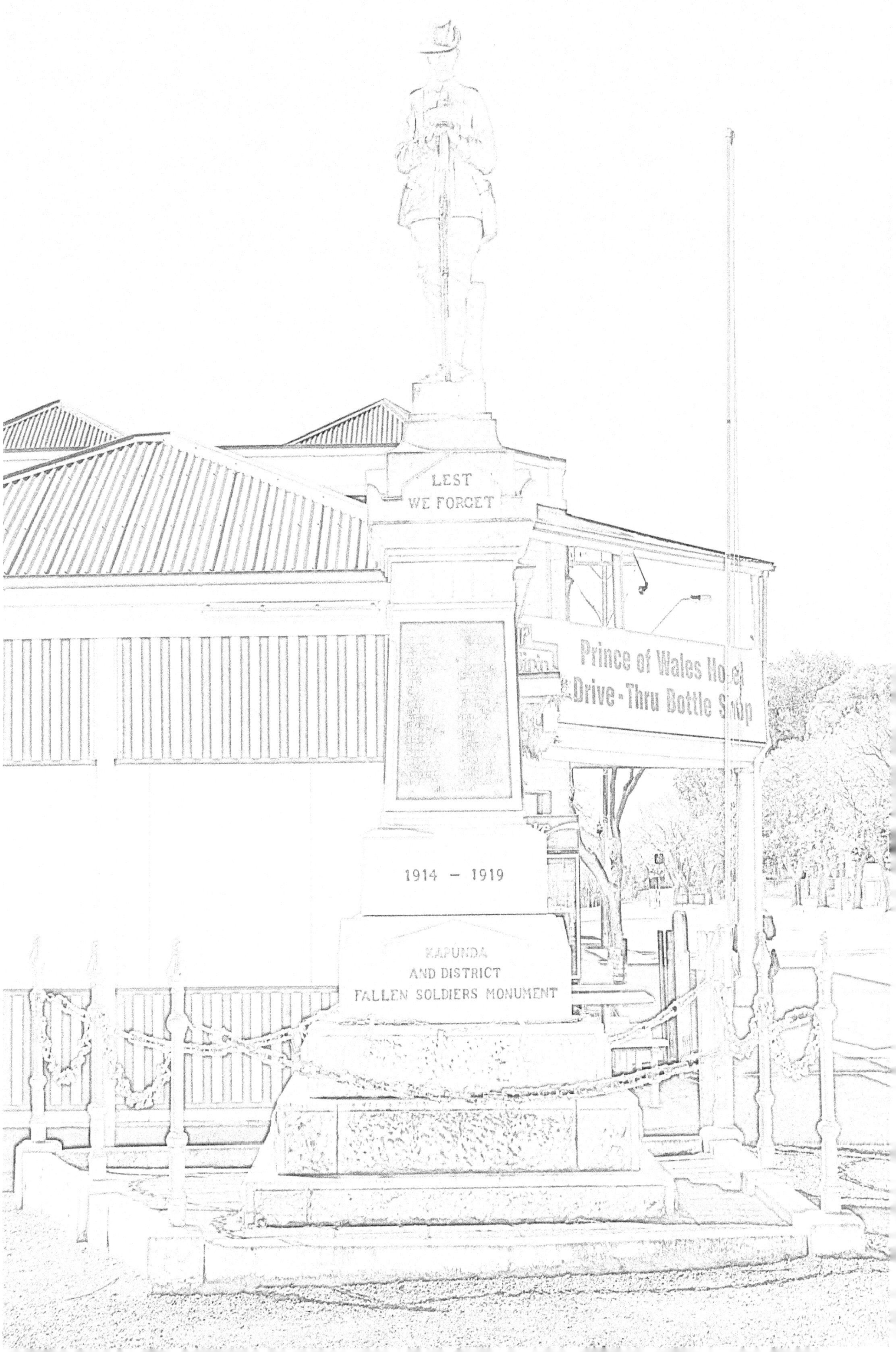
LEST
WE FORGET
1914 – 1919
KAPUNDA
AND DISTRICT
FALLEN SOLDIERS MONUMENT
Prince of Wales Ho
Drive-Thru Bottle S op

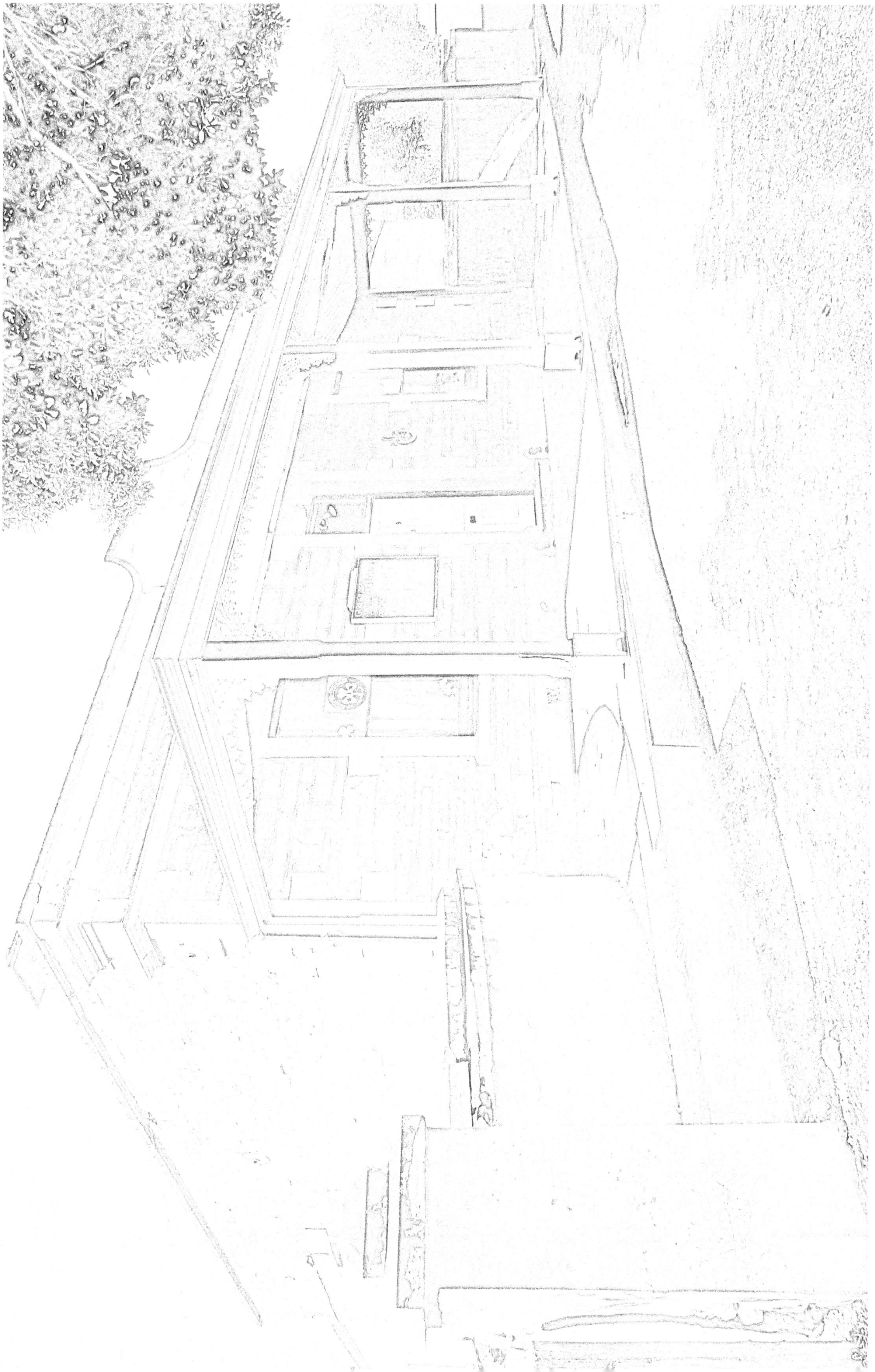

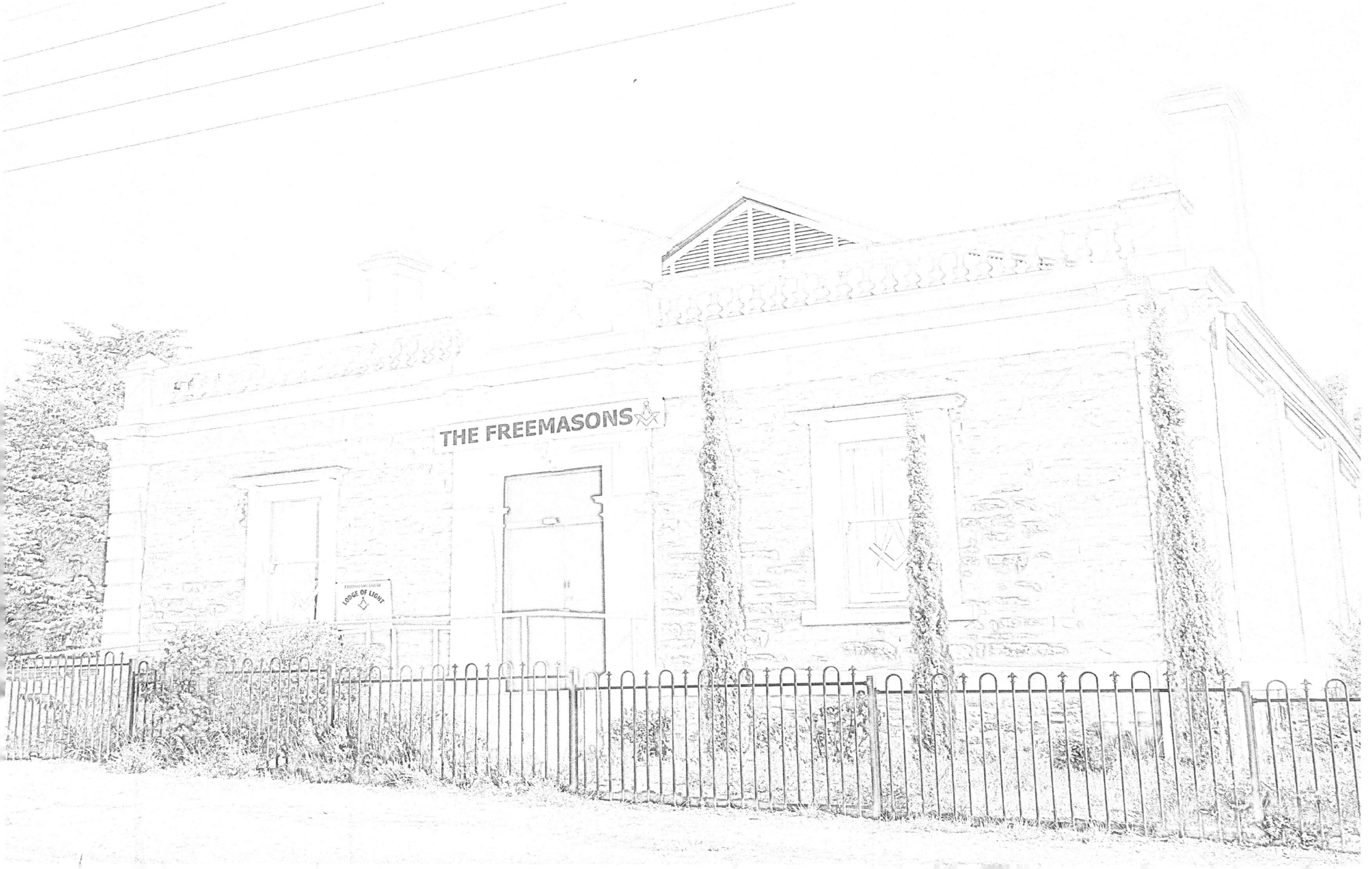
THE FREEMASONS
FREEMASONS LODGE
LODGE OF LIGHT

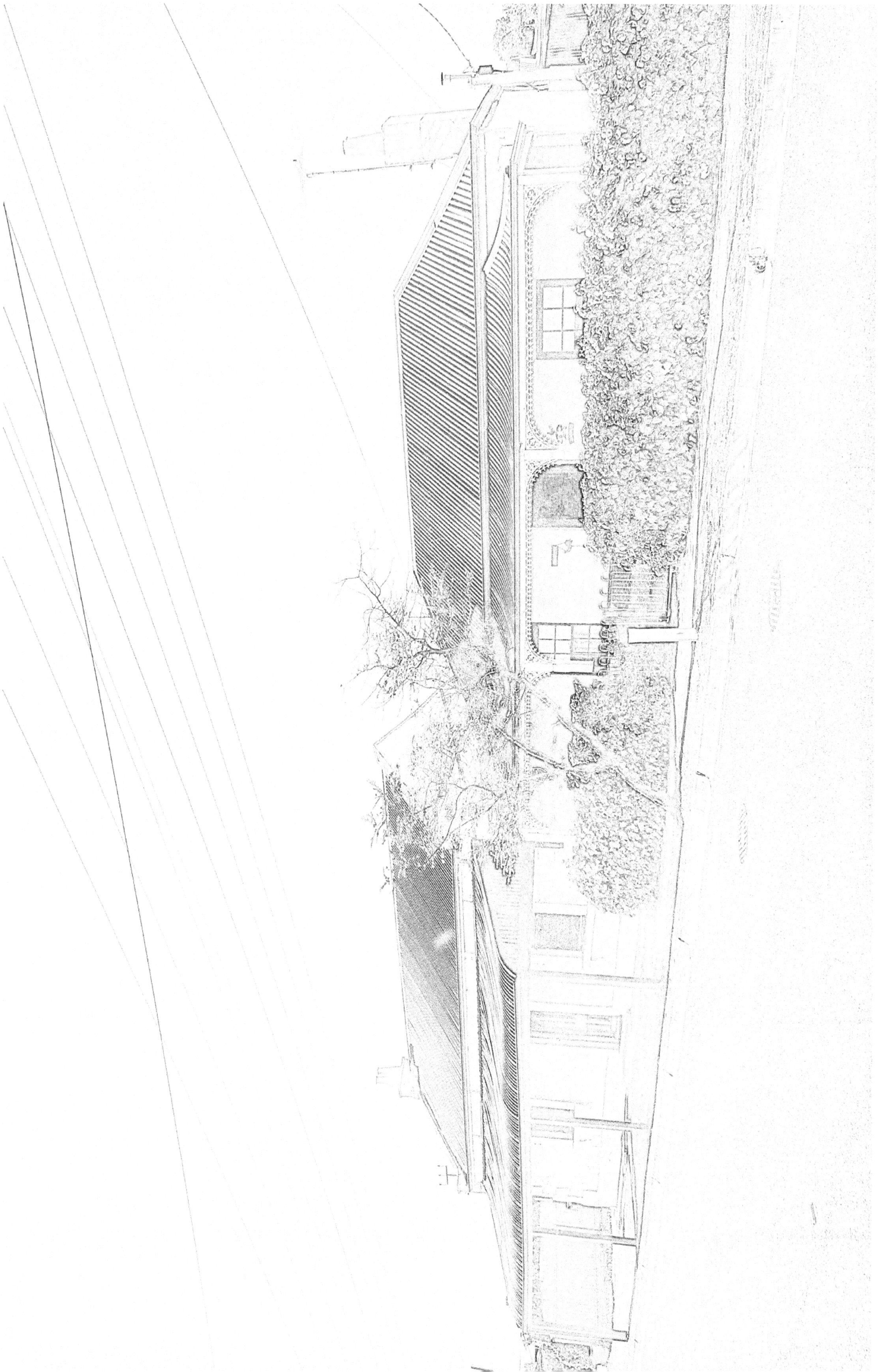

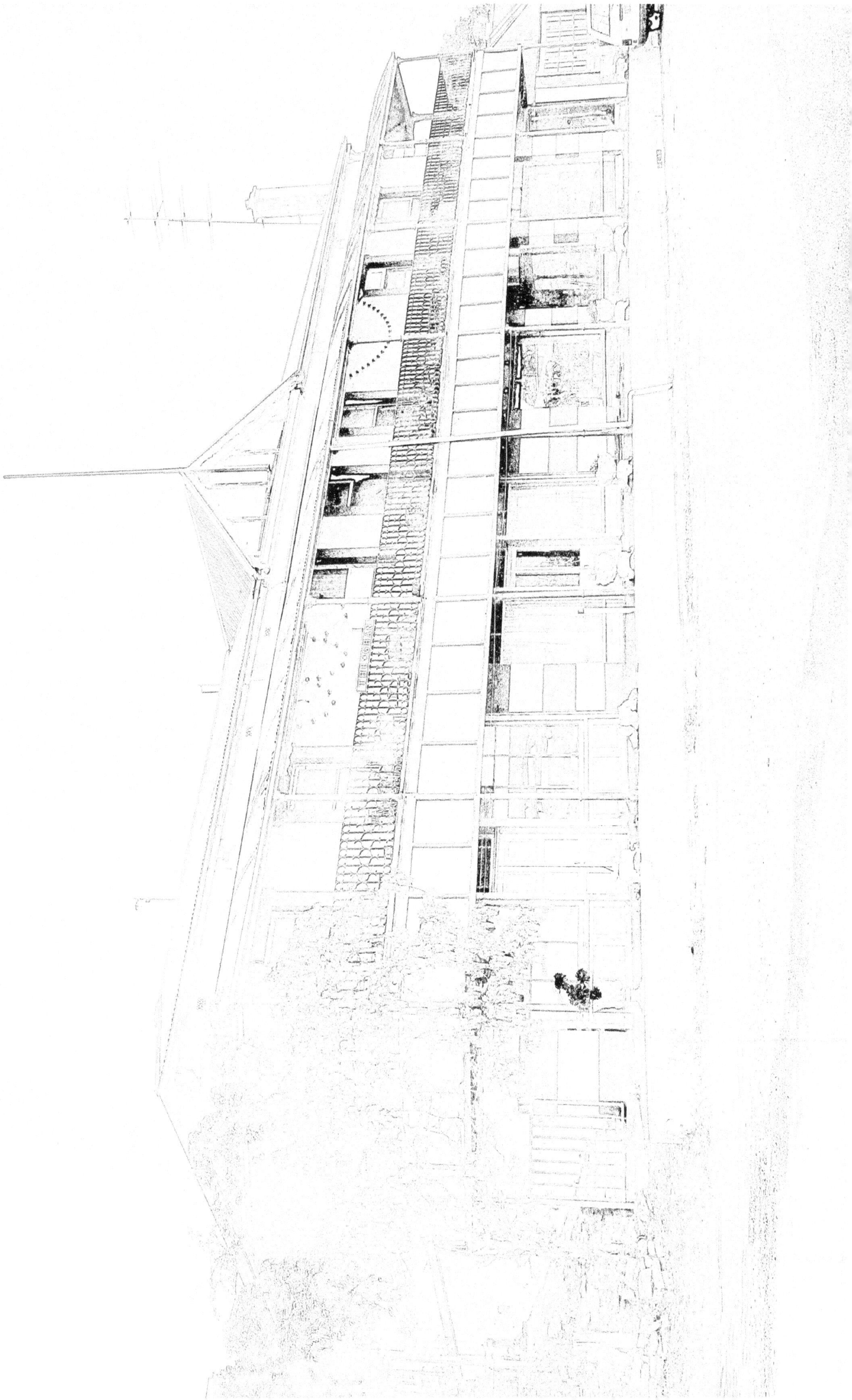

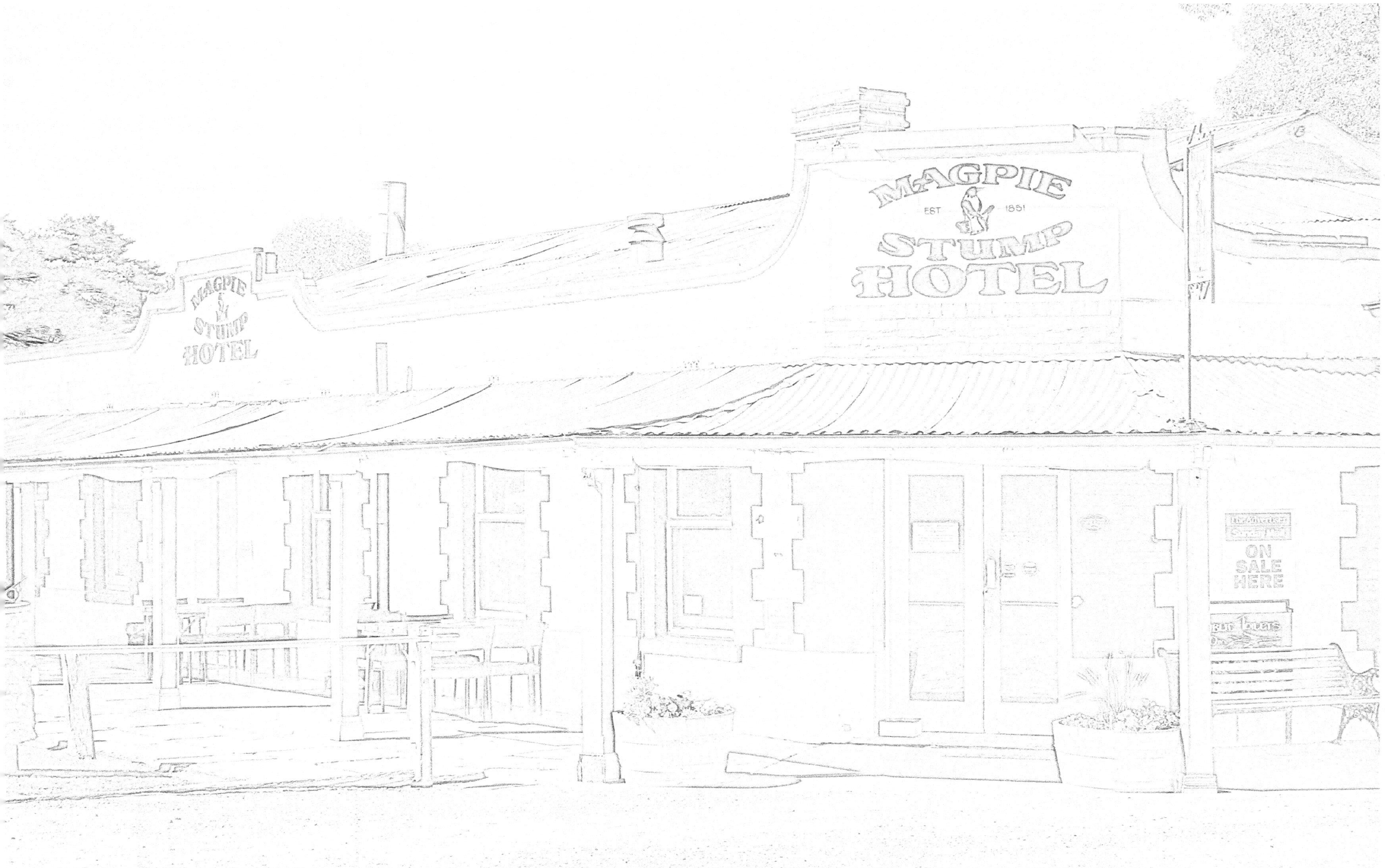
MAGPIE
EST 1851
STUMP
HOTEL
MAGPIE
STUMP
HOTEL
ON
SALE
HERE

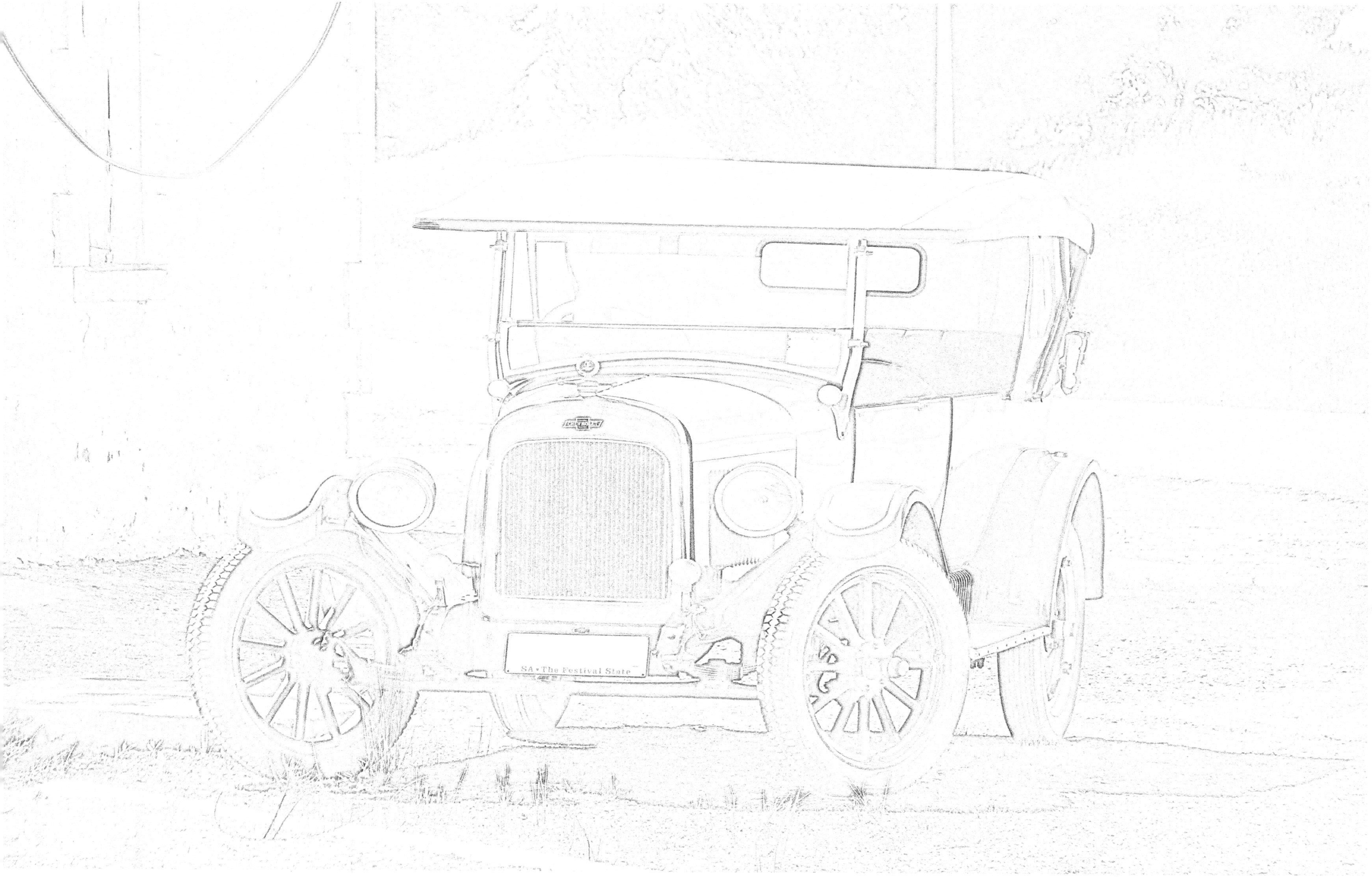
SA • The Festival State

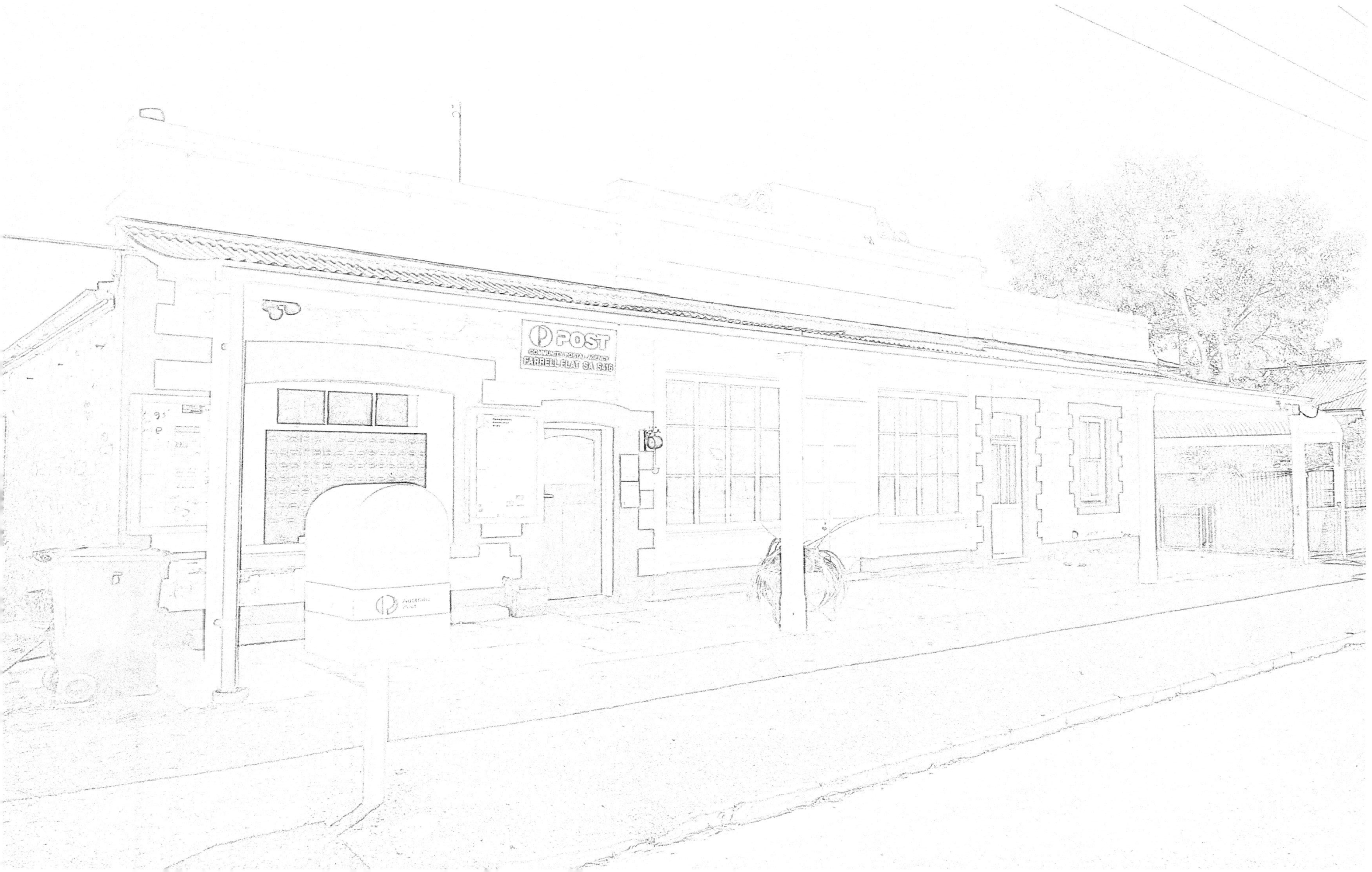
POST
COMMUNITY POSTAL AGENCY
FARRELL FLAT SA 5416

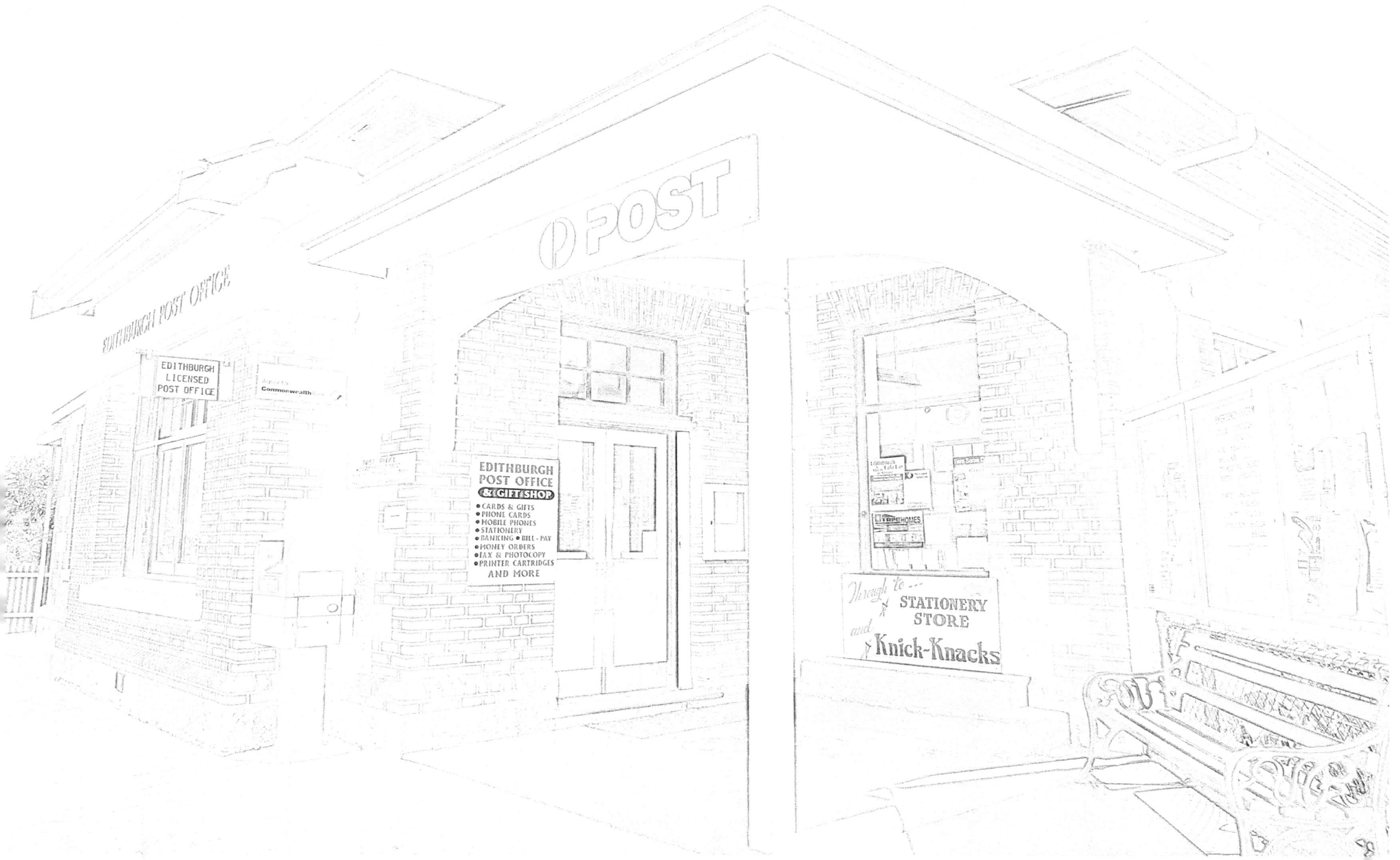
POST
EDITHBURGH POST OFFICE
EDITHBURGH
LICENSED
POST OFFICE
EDITHBURGH
POST OFFICE
& GIFT SHOP
CARDS & GIFTS
PHONE CARDS
MOBILE PHONES
STATIONERY
BANKING
BILL - PAY
MONEY ORDERS
FAX & PHOTOCOPY
PRINTER CARTRIDGES
AND MORE
Through to ...
STATIONERY
STORE
and
Knick-Knacks

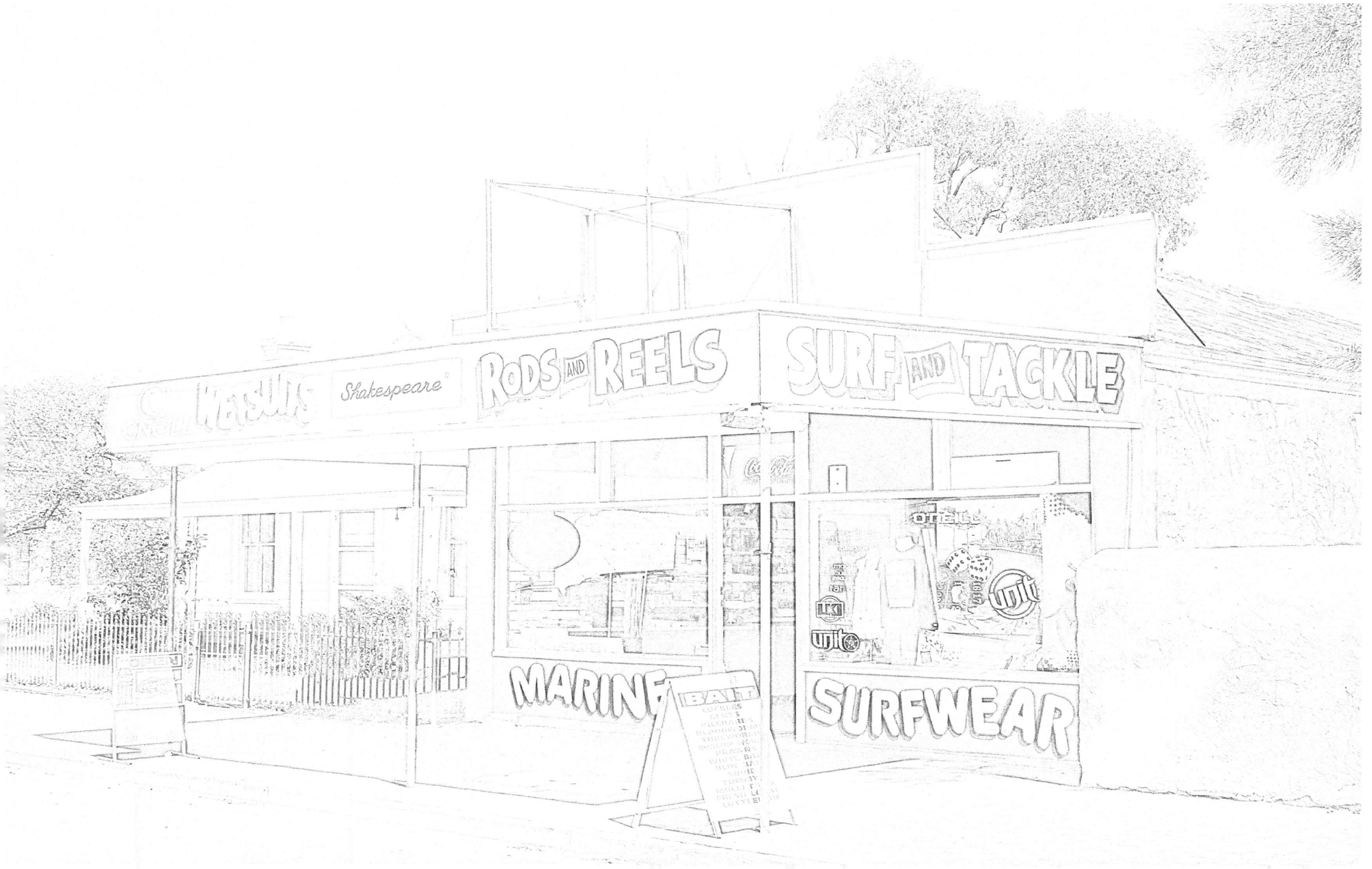
WETSUITS
Shakespeare
RODS AND REELS
SURF AND TACKLE
MARINE
BAIT
SURFWEAR

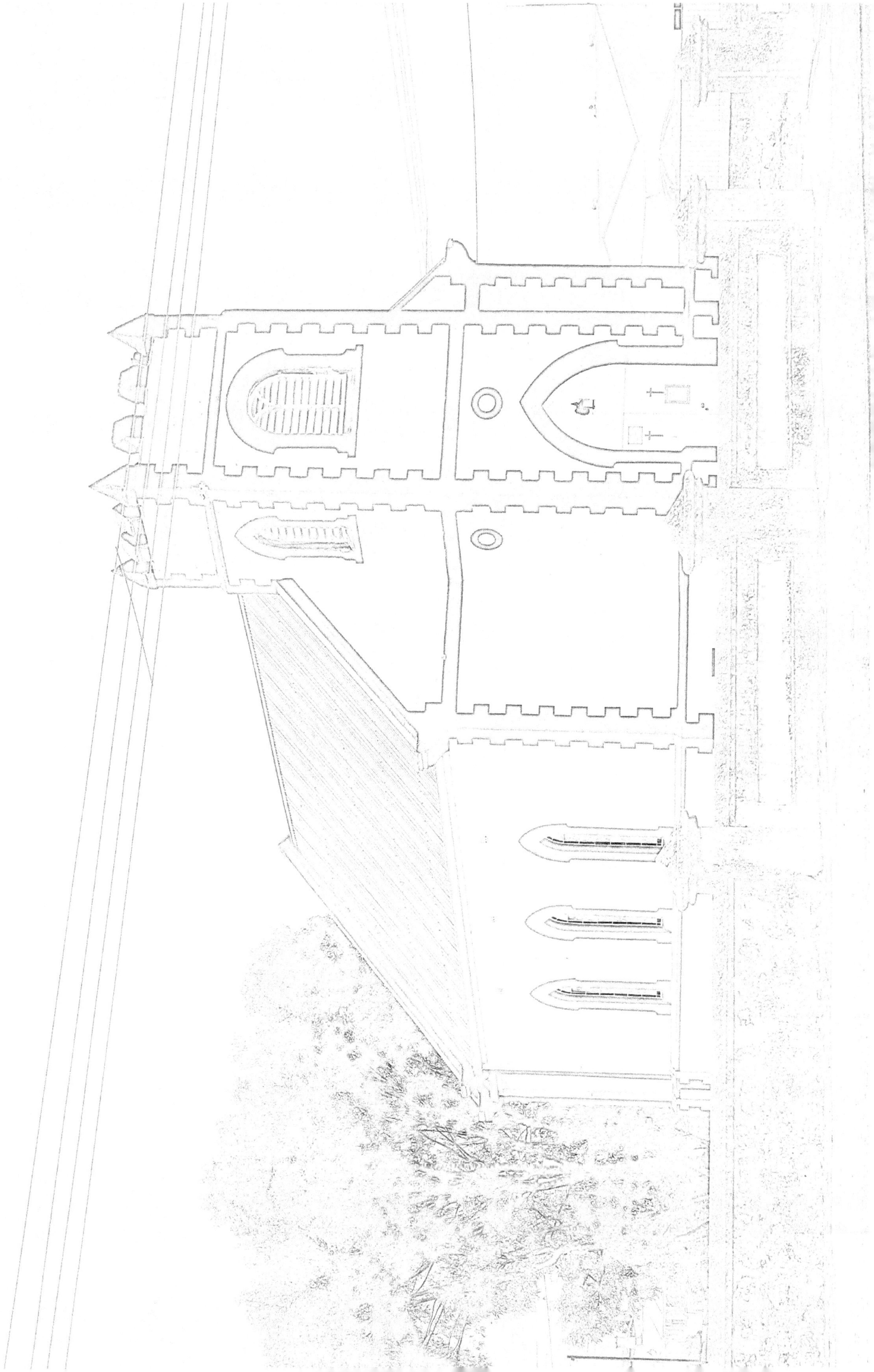

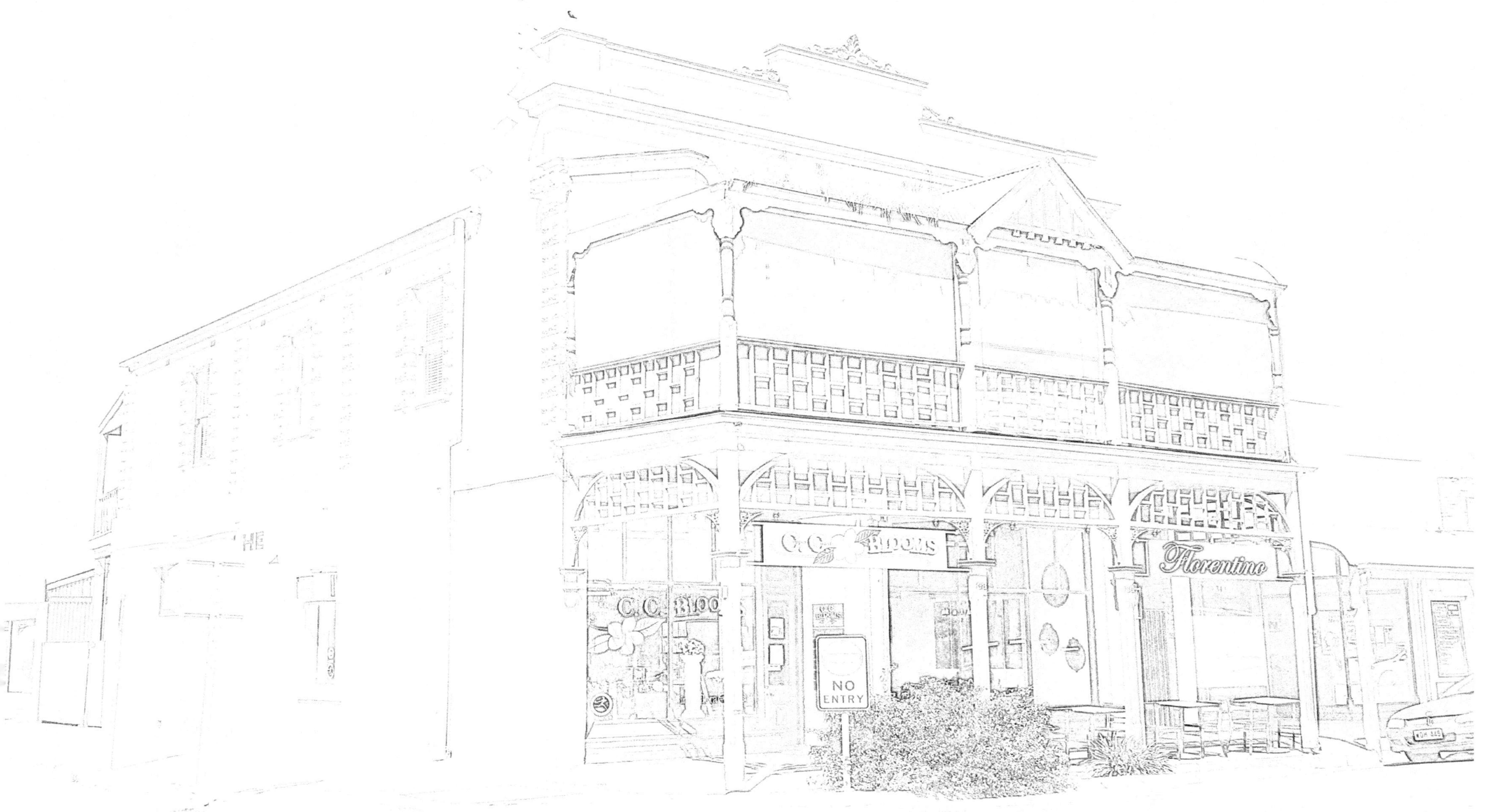
C.C. BLOOMS
Florentino
C.C. BLOO
NO ENTRY

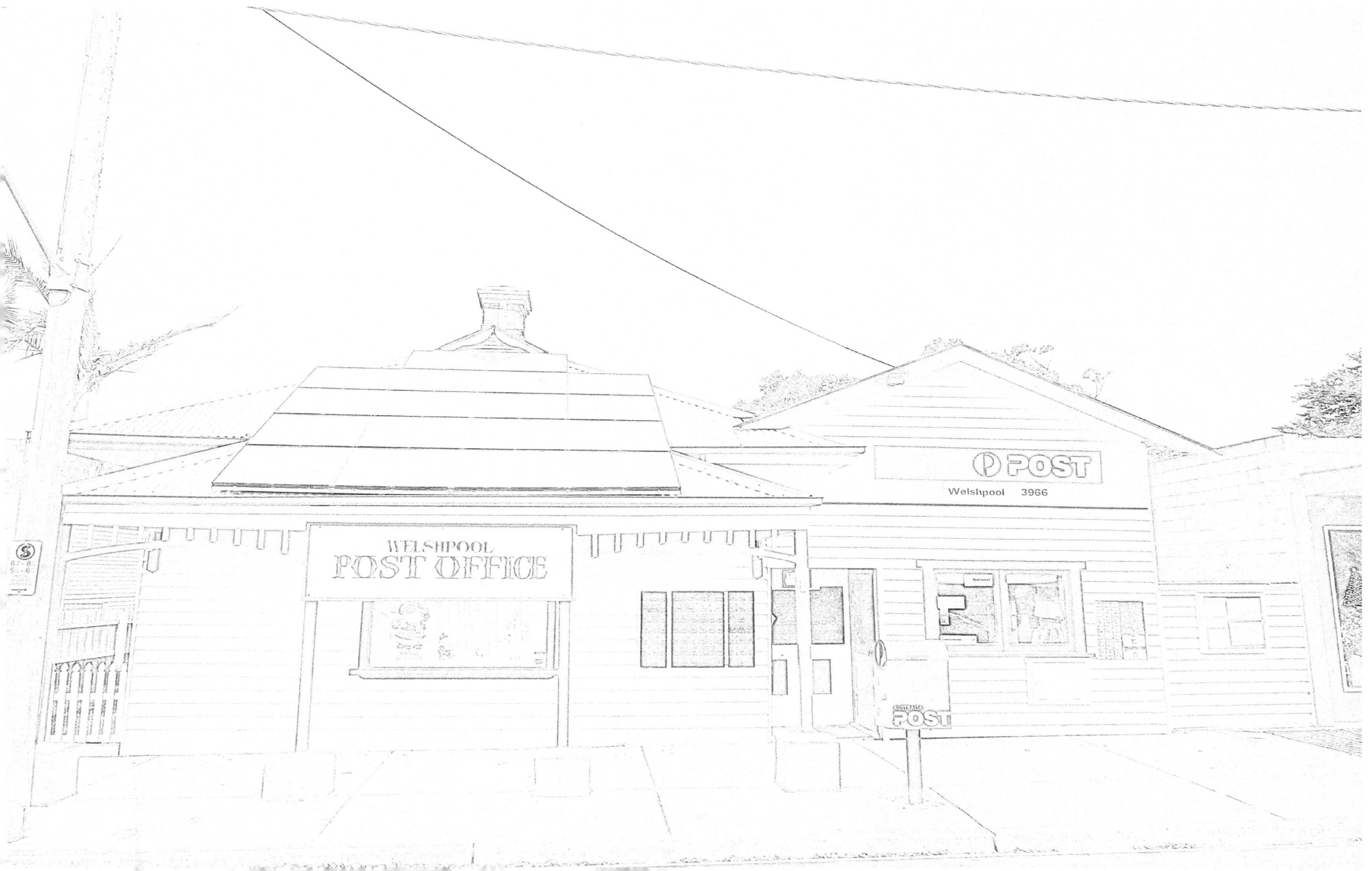
WELSHPOOL
POST OFFICE
POST
Welshpool 3966
POST

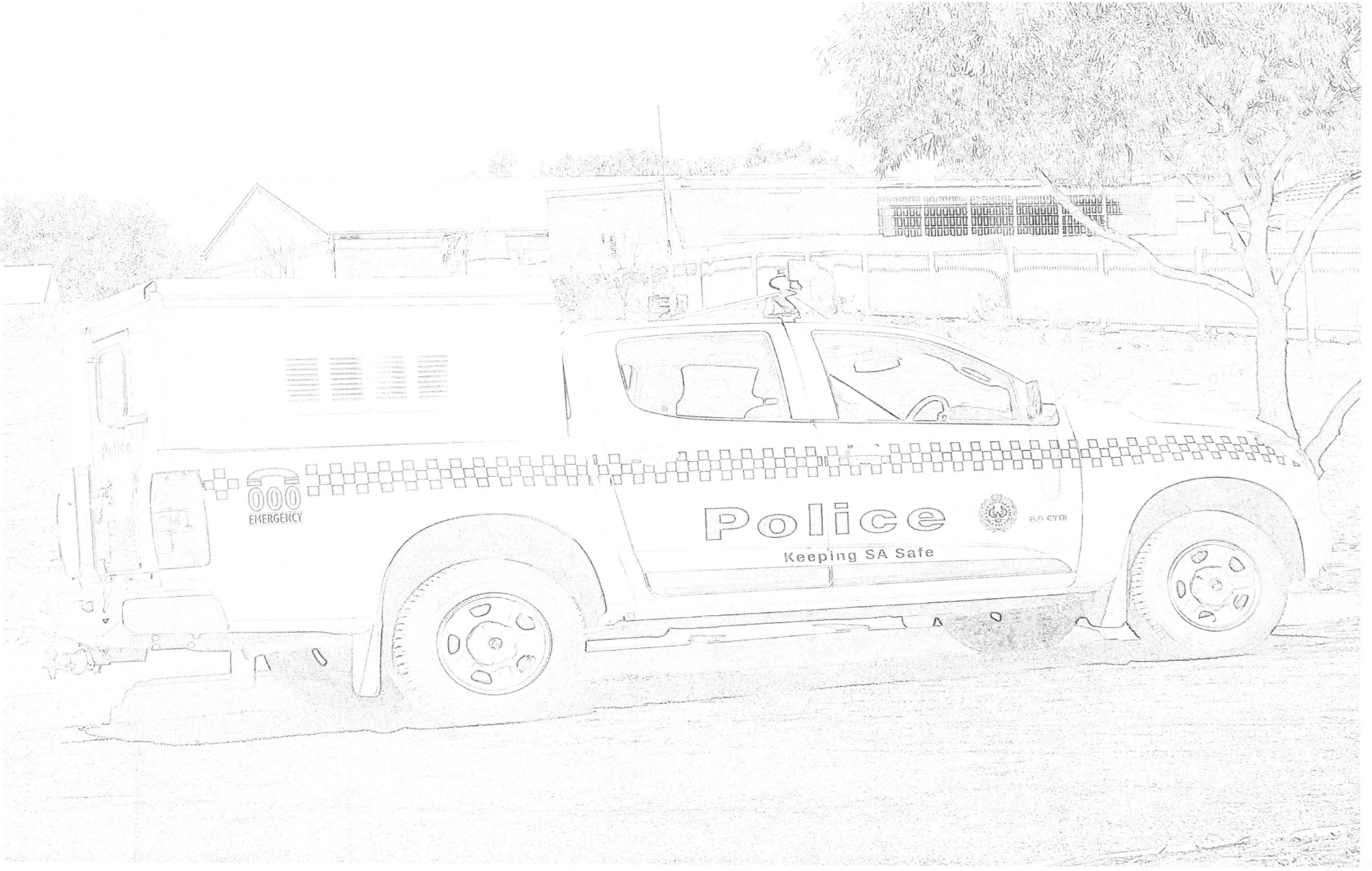

000
EMERGENCY
Police
Keeping SA Safe

www.ingramcontent.com/pod-product-compliance
Lightning Source LLC
Chambersburg PA
CBHW081059180526
45170CB00005B/1814